Singularities at the Threshold

Singularities at the Threshold

The Ontology of Unrest

Bruno Gullì

LEXINGTON BOOKS
Lanham • Boulder • New York • London

Published by Lexington Books
An imprint of The Rowman & Littlefield Publishing Group, Inc.
4501 Forbes Boulevard, Suite 200, Lanham, Maryland 20706
www.rowman.com

6 Tinworth Street, London SE11 5AL, United Kingdom

Copyright © 2020 by The Rowman & Littlefield Publishing Group, Inc.

All rights reserved. No part of this book may be reproduced in any form or by any electronic or mechanical means, including information storage and retrieval systems, without written permission from the publisher, except by a reviewer who may quote passages in a review.

British Library Cataloguing in Publication Information Available

Library of Congress Cataloging-in-Publication Data Is Available

Library of Congress Control Number: 2020945009

ISBN 978-1-7936-0676-1 (cloth: alk. paper)
ISBN 978-1-7936-0678-5 (pbk: alk. paper)
ISBN 978-1-7936-0677-8 (electronic)

For Pino, the most singular (in memory)

"Rien ne s'arrête pour nous . . . ; mais tout notre fondement craque, et la terre s'ouvre jusqu'aux abîmes" —Blaise Pascal

["Nothing rests for us . . . ; but our whole foundation cracks, and the earth opens into abysses" —my translation]

Contents

Introduction   1

1: Contingency   7
1. The Open: Ontology of Mystery and Simplicity   9
2. Replacing the Individual: The Impossible Individuation   23
3. Subject of Fiction: Subjection and Subjugation   37

2: Capture   51
4. Borders and Vortices (Life and Work)   53
5. Politics of Disposability and Cruelty   67
6. Capture and Thresholds: The Politics of Number, the Accidental Glass   83

3: Subversions   99
7. A Passage to Art   101
8. Disaffection and Care   119
9. Relations without a Subject   133

Bibliography   145
Index   151
About the Author   155

Introduction

This book intends to call into question the concept of the independent and sovereign individual of the liberal (and neoliberal) tradition. It does so by calling into question the politics of number from the point of view of the ontology of singularity. By ontology of singularity I mean the plural constitution of what appears to be *one*, an individual, a mere *this*. Singularity is not the result of a process of individuation. It is rather this very process itself. A process of individuation (whereby at each stage everything appears to be individuated as such, to be an individual thing), is in reality always already plural, a process of transindividuation, or better, as I will explain in the book, of *trans-dividuation*. For now, I can say that singularity is the name for this process; it is this plurality, which normally takes on the appearance of one, and then two, three, and so on. But singularity is plural in its very constitution, in its concept and unfolding, namely, in its ontology. Singularity is never simply one: this one and then another one, a second and third one, and so on. Singularity is not this one, but it is rather *thisness* with no one; it is less or more than a number, although it always appears and becomes fixed (normalized and stigmatized) as a number. Singularity is, then, not a borderline concept, like sovereignty, but a trans-conceptual reality providing the matrix for *this*(dis-)order, for difference without identity, relations without a subject, and being-with without number. Essentially, I will use the ontological notions of singularity and threshold to deconstruct the myth of the independent individual and address the question of what comes after sovereignty, the subject, and the politics of number.

The book is divided into three parts: Part One – Contingency; Part Two – Capture; Part Three – Subversions. Each part has three chapters, whose content I briefly describe below. Essentially, the book traces a trajectory from servitude to liberation insofar as the category of the independent and sovereign individual is seen as a normalizing/normalized abstraction (singularity in a cage) at all levels of existence, whereas singularities are seen in their complexity and multiplicity as a dynamic and open process of becoming, constantly gathering at the threshold of the common. Perhaps what characterizes the individual is loneliness, as well as a sad feeling of self-centeredness. But loneliness is pure fragmentation, alienation, disindividuation, ad disaffection; it is also a result of the illusion of independence. On the other hand, singularities, even in their solitude, are always open to a plurality of relations and to cooperation – even in their finitude, always infinitizing. This infinitizing process is what, in the last chapter of the book, I call *personality* (a schematism, or shadow, a glow or an aura) within singularity.

What makes the book singular in its own right is, I believe, the fact that it calls into question the politics of number and tries to distinguish between singularity and subjectivity. In fact, although much has been written on singularity, its usual conflation with subjectivity remains problematic and its meaning cannot become completely clear unless it is understood as a non-numerical, or nondenumerable, reality. Lately, all categories of identity, such as race, nationality, and gender, have been rightly called into question. Yet, to my knowledge, the category of number has not been given careful consideration. This book intends to do that. Indeed, becoming a number, being forced to be one, is perhaps the most effective way in which processes of normalization and stigmatization work. Becoming one necessarily entails the exclusion (really, the death) of the other.

Perhaps an analysis of singularity reveals that the individual, or the *one*, is never *there* as such, but that it is always a matter of dividuals, dividualities, fragments one might say, constituting a process of individuation that, however, remains open and never reaches the stage, or status, of the individual. In this sense, it is also interesting to note the difference between the concepts of individuation and individualization, of which Gilbert Simondon also speaks. The process of individuation, which never fully individuates, can also be understood, to use Leibniz's language against itself, as a multiplicity of predicates (or fragments) without a subject. As I mentioned above, singularity is this process itself. When one looks into singularity, one finds fragmented dividuals gathering at the threshold of the common, not independent and sovereign individuals. It is the gathering (*logos*) itself that constitutes the trans-dividual assemblage, network, or reality, which ultimately is what we are (and are not). In fact, independence does not obtain even for one moment or at any one stage of the process. There is always a degree of dependency, a notion I will take up again below. So perhaps transindividuality, a concept formulated by Gilbert Simondon, is not the best way to understand singularity. Perhaps one would have to speak of trans-dividuality rather than transindividuality. For this seems precisely to be the meaning of singularity. By saying this, I am not implying that transindividuality is a useless concept. In fact, it has been and still is very helpful in reformulating and calling into question categories of thought and reality. However, to my mind, singularity (or trans-dividuality) is a more radical concept. The question is not terminological, but conceptual and ontological. In fact, if the individual as such does not exist, how can anything be transindividual? Transindividuality seems to remain too close to interindividuality or intersubjectivity. Instead, everything is, in its very constitution, trans-dividual, and the singular names the process of trans-dividuality itself, its unfolding and becoming. It names the fragmentation and the difference – a difference without identity.

In his important book on transindividuality, *The Politics of Transindividuality* (2016), Jason Read says that the point is not demonstrating that everything is transindividual, but rather understanding the reasons for the effacement of the process of transindividuation itself. In other words, why does the individual appear as the main psychological, social, and political actor? Read repeatedly says that transindividuality is not the same as intersubjectivity, and that indeed it is completely different from it. In this sense, I believe that conceptually Read comes very close to the idea of singularity as trans-dividuality. Indeed, intersubjectivity names the modality of relation between independent individuals or subjects. Yet, the existential situation of dependency, or interdependence, by definition weakens the possibility of two fully independent and sovereign individuals establishing a relation with one another. I will use the concept of dependency a great deal in this work by relying particularly on the important book by Eva Feder Kittay, *Love's Labor: Essays on Women, Equality, and Dependency* (1999). Kittay shows how dependency is the inescapable fact of the human condition. There are stages in life of total (or almost total) dependency. However, even when that happens to a smaller degree and there is no full dependency, what one experiences is never total independence, but rather interdependence (or perhaps trans-dependence). It is interesting to note that few people (if any) would think of a situation of inter-independence – and the word, in fact, does not have much currency. Inter-independence sounds much like intersubjectivity, or inter-individuality, which even for Simondon is a "function of misrecognition."

I hope I have indicated the core themes of the book. In a snapshot, they are singularity, trans-dividuality, dependency, number, and personality. An important concept/metaphor I will regularly use is that of the gathering, or threshold, or gathering threshold. This is another way of speaking of singularity or trans-dividuality. The questions the book seeks to answer are: 1.) Why is singularity usually confused with individuality? The former is a wholly positive term and presents an ontology of multiplicity, a plural constitution, which is dynamic and open; the latter is the result of a negation and remains closed to new ontologies of constitutive relations. Singularity is the *constant crossing of the other into the other*. Even when we consider the 'same' existential reality, or what seems to be one individual entity, such crossing or passing over is constantly there – in such a way that the same is never truly and fully the same, but it is always different, even from itself. Individuality is the negation of that crossing, a sign of no trespassing. It is also the denumerable and serialized reality of number, of the crowd. Trans-dividuality, on the other hand, is the dialectical passage into a metastable difference; it is the negation of individuality, which is in turn the negation of dividuality; it is then the negation of the negation. 2.) What comes after the sovereign and independent individual, after the subject? The answer to this question is that it might perhaps be a matter of relations (or predicates) without a subject, the gathering of relations at the threshold. 3.) The passage to art and the new ontologies of plasticity (perhaps the posthuman) create the conditions for a new type of ethos and existence based on love and care rather than disaffection, loneliness, and disindividuation. What is the role of subversive and liberated singularities in bringing this about? In other words, what is the new composition of these *relations without a subject*? It is perhaps the truth of their (our) *uncontrollable* (Stiegler 2013) disposition, which is tired of quantification. In fact, quantifying is a matter (or task) of the police. But the method sought here must be Vico's method of transforming ourselves into the things and relations we are striving to become. It is a matter of experiencing existence as singularities at the gathering threshold of the common. However, without rejecting universality, following an insight by Giacomo Marramao (2012), we will speak of a *universalism of difference*.

It has not always been possible to be consistent with terminology. Thus, at times words like subject, individual, and self have been used in the traditional way, usually because they occurred in a quoted passage. But conceptually it should be kept in mind that we are here attempting a deconstruction of the paradigm of subjectivity, individuality, and selfhood – and that we try to do so, as much as possible, in a consistent way. It is for this reason that most of the times we prefer the neutral pronoun 'it' for subject, individual, and so on.

The first chapter deals with a cluster of related concepts: the open, contingency, mystery, and simplicity. It does so by looking at the thought of Laozi and Zhuangzi, two ancient Chinese Taoist philosophers, but it then also considers, among the others, Leibniz, the thinker of contingency, and Gaston Bachelard on the dialectic of the open. The point is to give an account of singularity from the point of view of contingency, namely, against any essentialism, but according to a dynamic philosophy of the accidental and the ontology of plurality. Marramao's concept of universalism of difference is also treated here.

Chapters Two and Three present a critique of the concepts of the individual and the subject. The claim about the possibility of replacing the individual, made in Chapter Two, may at first sight appear a bit too strong and perhaps unrealistic. Yet, first of all, at one point Simondon himself suggests it, and then, fundamentally, it is obvious that an analysis of individuation reveals that individuation as such, as a completed process, is impossible. Rather, the *individuating* process remains open; hence, the individual is not even a stage in it, but the appearance of a phase in what Simondon calls the "theater of individuation." Chapter Three involves a critical analysis of the metaphysics of subjectivity according to the twofold mode of subjection and subjugation. What will become clear is that even subjectivation remains within that metaphysical paradigm, and that, as such, it cannot be an alternative to subjection. The real alternative to subjection, and to the whole metaphysics of subjectivity, is singularity.

Chapters Four, Five, and Six deal with the general question of capture in terms of the border, work, extreme violence, the politics of number (biopolitics), and, as an exit from capture, the possibility of the threshold. In Chapter Four there is a discussion of the modes of digital technology, both in relation to servitude and liberation. Chapter Five treats the issues of disposability, waste, and exterminism, among other things. Chapter Six in particular focuses on the concept of threshold and the ontology of the accident. Chapters Seven, Eight, and Nine attempt to describe a trajectory of subversions through the thresholds of art and labor, disaffection and care, and finally the mode of relations without a subject.

1

Contingency

ONE

The Open

Ontology of Mystery and Simplicity

In *The Passage West*, Giacomo Marramao speaks of "the theoretical program of a *universalism of difference*" (2012: 16) as a prescriptive transfiguration (and reconceptualization) of cosmopolitanism and modernity. In an important paragraph at the outset of his book, he says, "Once we have left behind us the *discordia concors* between the individualist-market homologation thesis and that of the clash of civilisations, globalization will reveal its true character. Not as the 'Westernization of the world',[1] nor as 'de-Westernization' and 'desecularization', but as the *passage to the Occident* of all cultures. That is, a passage to modernity destined to produce profound transformations in the economy, society, lifestyles and codes of behaviour not only of 'other' civilisations but of Western civilisation itself" (15). This is a very interesting thesis, which reveals the character of the open and contingent, as well as that of the cultural paradigm of trans-dividuality. In a sense, this changes everything because it very explicitly unearths the constant interpenetration of cultures and civilizations and gives a new orientation to thinking. The process has been ongoing for a long time, certainly since the beginning of modernity, but in many ways even before that. Yet, it now reaches an undeniable, or at least more evident, configuration. Marramao says, "The more modernity expands, spreading the economics and aesthetics of the commodity on a global scale, the more Western society is permeated by cultural 'alterity'" (*ibid.*). Thus, he highlights "the *pluriversal nature of the process of civilisation and the plurality of the possible paths towards modernity*" (*ibid.*; emphasis in the original). Using Niklas Luhmann's notion of 'world-society' (*Weltgellschaft*) and its "asynchronic development" and asymptotic movement toward a new unity, Marramao understands the *"new map of the world . . .*

in the light of the complex and problematic character of the distinction between the global and the local" (27). This is, he says, the *form* of what we call 'globalization' (*ibid.*). Indeed, with a reference to Roland Robertson, he puts the accent on the *glocal* and *glocalization*. This new form is for Marramao "the global institutionalisation of the lifeworld and the localisation of globality" (*ibid.*). This never happens as a mere juxtaposition and proximity of the global and the local, but rather as their constant and paradoxical co-presence and co-belonging (28–29). Marramao very clearly says that the term 'glocal' "designates the fusing together of the two, intimately interwoven movements of the globalisation of the local and the localisation of the global" (35).

It is by way of the preceding remarks on Marramao's work that I want to turn to the philosophy of Laozi, whom Marramao refers to in his book as well. With a reference to Karl Jaspers and his celebrated thesis of the 'axial period' in world history and philosophy, Marramao shows how the Orient/Occident opposition, with the consequent notion of a European exception, is really "a macroscopic case of 'imagined community'" (51). As Marramao explains, Jaspers' thesis, advanced in 1949 in *The Origin and Goal of History*, "situated the axis of world history in a 'global transformation of human-being' that took place sometime between 800 and 200 B.C., with the years around 500 B.C. as the critical period" (47–48). He continues, "It is possible to observe, at this time, in the 'three worlds' of India, China and the Occident (a term inclusive of Greece but also of ancient Palestine), a synchronic passage from mythical to rational thought, from *mythos* to *logos*" (48). However, despite Jaspers' thesis (and despite Edward Said's later deconstruction of the concept of the 'Orient' in *Orientalism*), we usually find an engagement with the work of thinkers like Laozi, or the Daoist tradition in general, only when dealing with comparative philosophy or religion: with, precisely, the Orient/Occident, or East/West, dyad. Thus, interest in traditions that, from the viewpoint of Western thinking (European and Anglo-American), are seen as 'others,' remains marginal, a supplement to the 'real' issue or central point – or even worse, marketed as a New Age mode of thinking and lifestyle. In a sense, this is the same as the discourse on art, which, unless one deals with it in its specificity, is seen as marginal to the general discourse of philosophy and theory – a supplement, again, as Lewis Mumford (2000) said. In truth, the alternative is not to reiterate once again the paradigm of the same and the other (as if the other were not also the same, and the same the other). The real alternative is to explode the whole paradigm and enter – perhaps invent – a different one, in which the question of the same and the other no longer applies: a *universalism of difference*, as Marramao suggests, as well as a *glocal* experience of the philosophical.

I have decided to include a discussion of themes from the *Daodejing* in this chapter because they are central to a phenomenological inquiry into contingency and the open, as well as to the inquiry into singularities and gathering thresholds, the theme of the book. The ontology of mystery and simplicity, also in the title of this chapter, is central to the themes of contingency and the open. It provides a structural formula for a reading of passages from the *Daodejing*, but it also points to other important experiences in philosophy; for instance, it points to the work of Gottfried Wilhelm Leibniz and John Duns Scotus (and through the latter to the Franciscan tradition as a whole). There are of course many translations of Laozi's book, at times very different from one another. I will be quoting from the version by Philip J. Ivanhoe, but I may rely on other versions as well, in particular the one by Julius Lodewijk Duyvendak.

The first, famous line of the *Daodejing* says, "A Way that can be followed is not a constant Way." The second line, parallel to the first, says, "A name that can be named is not a constant name." They both immediately introduce the problem of permanence and change central to all metaphysical traditions; in fact, to reality as such. The Way is hidden, and yet manifest; it is the same and not the same. Sameness, or identity, is also the theme of the second line. The unnamed name, that is, the constant name, is the singularity of a thing. To name is to identify something, namely, to claim for it a condition of identity, which always displaces its singularity; it de-singularizes it, reducing it to the status of a number, or its proximity. The constant Way cannot be followed, and the constant name cannot be named. Yet, following and naming are part of the unfolding of the Power (*De*) of the Way (*Dao*) – thresholds or paths into the open and contingent. Way (*Dao*) really means 'what is on the way,' and Power (*De*) is the potency whereby 'what is on the way' stays its course and abides in its endless flow or state of unrest. As such, they are inevitable modalities of existence, or modes of being. There is an apparent dualism in the concept of the Way, as well as in that of the name, a twofold structure. Yet, this apparent duality does not separate two irreducible ontological planes, as is the case in other traditions – traditions of transcendence. Rather, we find here a solid and clear paradigm of immanence. The mystery/manifestation dyad can be understood as being very similar to Spinoza's celebrated description of nature as *natura naturans* and *natura naturata*. In Spinoza, too, there is no dualism, but different expressions of the same singularity. For Laozi, permanence persists within change; the hidden Way is the same (and not the same), as are its manifestations; the unnamed remains within the named, constantly calling into question (and really threatening) its spurious and shaky identity. In fact, contingency is not in the accidental, but in what causes it. The open will not be found in the total absence of borders, but in their vacillation, as Étienne Balibar notes (Balibar 2002: 88–92), and in the open's own reservoir of potency and projectuality, a cipher of the *not-yet*. But what is the name of the Way? How are we to address it? As Laozi, the semilegendary author of the *Daodejing* says, "I do not know its proper name; / I have styled it 'the Way'" (Chapter 25). Thus, it is the open. In this same chapter, we read that the Way, in its unfolding, goes far, and in going far, it "returns to its source" (*ibid.*). Its singularity, which cannot be named or numbered, describes an asymptotic movement toward an impossible individuation, and ultimately not a return to itself, which is equally impossible, but a revolutionary passage to simplicity, contamination – in the sense spoken about by Kwame Anthony Appiah (2006) and Jacques Derrida (1988) – and the tension between finitude and infinitude. In the last chapter of this book, we will link this description of the Way to Nishida Kitarō's idea of the mediation of the continuity of discontinuity (Nishida 2012). As Paul-Antoine Miquel says in a recent book on the relationship between humans and the biosphere, "Le tout est en effet ouvert sur lui-même" ["The whole is in fact open over itself"] (2019: 42; emphasis removed).[2] Miquel says this with a reference to Gilbert Simondon's concept of the pre-individual, which addresses the question of the potential, and a reference to Lucretius' idea of the immensity of the open (the universe), which is "neither a complete plenum nor a complete vacuum" (Lucretius 2001: 16). Thus, the open, the universe or multiverse, the whole is "an identity of re-totalization, whereby it returns to what it had initially been" (Miquel 2019: 42). Obviously, the concept of identity here includes that of difference; re-totalization and return follow the asymptotic movement I mentioned above, which leads toward an impossible individuation, and impossible closed totality. The pre-individual remains open and incomplete not "because it lacks something that it might acquire"; rather, it is "structurally, or in other words ontologically incomplete, structurally defined by a lack, by the absence of foundation" (*ibid.*). The twofold, immanent structure of the Way, its unfolding movement, represents precisely this moment of open self-differentiation and impossible individuation. As the key to a reading of the *Daodejing*, this structure is clearly announced at the end of Chapter One in the opposition/distinction (in unity) of mysteries and manifestations: "These two come forth in unity but diverge in name. / Their unity is known as an enigma. / Within this enigma is yet a deeper enigma. / The gate of all mysteries!" The idea of the interconnectedness of all things is found here, but also the characteristic structure and dynamic process of the Way, its unending unfolding, its being at the same time concealed and manifest.

The central Daoist concept is that of *nonaction* (*wu wei*). As a long tradition of exegesis within sinology has demonstrated, nonaction is not at all pure passivity, not doing anything, but rather *effortless* action, namely, not doing too much, not overdoing something. It is not simply *wu wei*, not doing, but *wei wu wei*, the doing of not doing. Indeed, as we read so often in the *Daodejing*, the wise person engages in the doing of not doing, acts without acting – just as the best way of teaching is by not teaching at all and of ruling by not ruling, according to Zhuangzi, another extremely important Daoist thinker. Thus, "Sages enact nonaction and everything becomes well ordered" (Chapter Three). This idea is in keeping with the very movement of the Way itself and what is perhaps the most central line, the most central teaching of Laozi's book, "The Way does nothing yet nothing is left undone" (Chapter Thirty-seven). Humans should act accordingly and do the same, "One does less and less until one does nothing; / One does nothing yet nothing is left undone" (Chapter Forty-eight). When we consider this in the context of today's obsession with speed, productivity, and possession, the injunction to work and be competitive and succeed, with all the consequences that this attitude has, from anxiety to capture, from servitude to poverty, we realize how fruitful it is to listen to it. Reading a book like the *Daodejing* is then not, as is often assumed, an exercise in some type of New Age spirituality, or similar practices; it is rather a confrontation with a deeply materialist and immanentist conception of the world. Indeed, *wei wu wei* (the doing of not doing) can very well be understood as an *ante litteram* formulation of the *refusal to work*, theorized and practiced by the Italian autonomist movement. Furthermore, as I already mentioned in an article I wrote many years ago, there may be other interesting applications of Laozi's (and Zhuangzi's) concept to our contemporary thinking and concerns. This is a modified quote from that article: "At the end of a brief, but dense and interesting, article on some thematic correspondences between Gramsci and Buddhism, Giangiorgio Pasqualotto applies the Daoist concept of *wei wu wei* to Gramsci's philosophy of praxis, to his theory of the action which entails, not a frontal and rigid opposition to the enemy, but the ability to draw the enemy into ruin on the basis of the enemy's own force. This is done, Pasqualotto says, by means of a 'non passive patience' (a Buddhist concept similar to the Daoist concept of *wu wei*), which is a characteristic of the will, and which has the form of a capacity of resistance (Pasqualotto, 452–456)" (Gullì 2005a: 183).

My reference to the will in relation to Gramsci is to the rational, concrete, will, which for Gramsci must be put "at the basis of philosophy" (Gramsci 1971: 345). For Gramsci, this rational (and not arbitrary) will "in the last analysis equals practical or political activity" (*ibid.*). Gramsci speaks of this in the context of the question, "What is philosophy?" (*ibid.*). His answer is that philosophy, the philosophy of praxis, is a situational *creative* activity – creative in a relative (i.e., not absolute or speculative) sense. In particular, Gramsci understands the word 'relative' in a trans-dividual sense, namely, "as thought which modifies the way of feeling of many and consequently reality itself, which cannot be thought without this many" (346). The reference to 'the many,' as well as to reality as a whole, can today be understood as a reference to the multitude and the network. For Gramsci, this is, moreover, "an historical relationship" (*ibid.*). Thus, the word 'creative' points to the trans-dividual (transductive) *and* dialectical making of reality. In this sense, it reaches into the open and potential. However, the potential here must be understood in its full form of contingency, as including the potentiality-not-to, namely, the doing of not doing, the Daoist *wei wu wei*. This is included both in the infinitizing finitude of trans-dividuality and in the movement through negation of the dialectic. The question is not simply that of reproducing reality, but rather that of creatively reshaping it, on the basis of the ruin of the enemy. It is a transformed and transfigured reality that the philosophy of praxis brings about; this is what the concrete and rational will aims at – by including, to be sure, the potentiality-not-to, an apparently passive force capable of imploding or exploding the positions of the enemy, both war of position and war of maneuver.

The doing of not doing is not doing nothing at all, just like nothing is not nothing in an absolute sense, for the simple fact that absolute nothing is impossible, as a whole tradition of metaphysics, from Parmenides to Leibniz and beyond, shows. In one of the most important chapters of the *Daodejing*, Chapter Eleven, which I quote in its entirety, we can precisely appreciate the importance of negation and emptiness: "Thirty spokes are joined in the hub of a wheel. / But only by relying on what is not there, do we have the use of the carriage. / By adding and removing clay we form a vessel. / But only by relying on what is not there, do we have use of the vessel. / By carving out doors and windows we make a room. / But only by relying on what is not there, do we have use of the room. / And so, what is there is the basis for profit; / What is not there is the basis for use" (Laozi 2002: 21). Laozi goes back many times to the opposition between profit and use, or possession and use. Use, or consumption, just like production, engages the negative. Possession, or profit, completely disregards it. In the latter case, we have a disfiguration of the real. In the former, we have its transfiguration, its passage into the open and contingent. The opposition between what is and what is not, being and (relative) nothing, their distinction in unity (or better, in singularity), common to the dialectic from Heraclitus to Hegel and to the yin-yang dialectic of Daoism, yields the concept of becoming or change, and with it the vacillating process of trans-dividuation. However, the stress must be on the negative and precisely on what yields. In the being-with of singularity, it is always a moment of absence, *wu wei*, an empty space, which holds things together in a dynamic fashion. Fixation, that ultimate form of passivity, is avoided, and contingency remains in operation, the open stays open. This is the meaning of the following lines from Chapter Ten of the *Daodejing*, "To produce without possessing; / To act with no expectation of reward; / To lead without lording over" (20). Indeed, domination, status, and possession are forms of fixation and capture, and they are passive modes. On the other hand, production (and, obviously, consumption), action, and undertaking a new path, namely, experiencing (which is what leading is), are dynamic and creative modes of existence. This is Laozi's ontology of mystery and simplicity.

In relation to the question of simplicity, we can look at what is perhaps, at the interpretive level, the most controversial chapter of the *Dao-*

dejing, Chapter Eighty, its penultimate chapter. This chapter is also important in relation to the notion of the 'glocal' we mentioned above. I will not quote the whole chapter here, but I will choose a few of the most significant lines, as the tone of the whole chapter is consistent with them. In what seems to be a piece of advice to a potential ruler, an endeavor typical of Confucius and other philosophers in ancient China before its unification by Qin Shi Huangdi in 221 BC, Laozi says, "Reduce the size of the state; / Lessen the population" (83). Obviously, Laozi's ruler is, if anything, one who rules by not ruling. Here, too, not ruling is not complete inaction, but it is rather the implementation of not ruling in accordance with the Way. In fact, we can assume that Laozi is not addressing a ruler at all, but the general question of how to conduct life, at the personal and collective level. It is perhaps a loose notion of governance, certainly not ruling as domination, sovereignty, or lording over, that we find here; to use Michel Foucault's terminology and concepts, it is not the government of others, but the government of self, and thus the care of the self. Yet, it is always a type of care emerging from the doing of not doing and from a stance of refusal. The case was completely different with Confucius, for whom it was important to conform to the rule, at the personal and collective level and ultimately to give an orderly and hierarchical structure to an eventually unified China. Indeed, for Confucius (2000), the Way (*Dao*) was to be based on rites (*li*) and humanness (*ren*). For Confucius, governing (and caring for) oneself, but also others, will yield the *Junzi*, or person of excellence (often translated as gentleman or superior man), and it ultimately will guarantee order and stability at the political and social level. Laozi's advice, as is always the case with him, points to negation and letting go as a way of attaining, not order, but harmony. Yet, it has nothing to do with the notion of less government of some conservative ideologies of our own age. Instead, it is a reference to his general philosophy of anarchy, found throughout the *Daodejing* and typical of the Daoist tradition as a whole. The Daoist sage, in a way similar to Herman Melville's Bartleby and his "I would prefer not to," will rather stay in the doing of not doing. This is the meaning of the story about Zhuangzi (Chuang Tzu) in Chapter 17, "Season of Autumn Floods," of his book: Zhuangzi was fishing when two senior officials from the State of Chu came along to tell him that the King wanted him to take care of the administration of his land. The story says that Zhuangzi went on fishing and replied as follows, "I hear that in Chu there is a sacred tortoise which died three thousand years ago. The King keeps this in his ancestral temple, wrapped and enclosed. Tell me, would this tortoise have wanted to die and leave his shell to be venerated? Or would he rather have lived and continued to crawl about in the mud?" Obviously, the officials reply that the tortoise "would rather have lived and continued to crawl about in the mud." Zhuangzi then asks them to go away, "I will continue to crawl about in the mud!" (Chuang Tzu 2006: 147). To go back to Chapter Eighty of the *Daodejing* in light of the passage by Zhuangzi, it is easy to see how a compelling interpretation of this chapter is precisely in line with a philosophy of refusal and the doing of not doing. Laozi says, "Even though they [people, the multitude] have ships and carts, they will have no use for them. / Even though they have armor and weapons, they will have no reason to deploy them" (brackets added). This is not a call to a time of stagnation, but rather to the leisure of 'wagging one's tail in the mud,' as Zhuangzi and his tortoise do – a time in which we do not shorten what is long and do not lengthen what is short. Yet, it is a time for theory and praxis. There are projects and things made: "Make their food savory, / Their clothes fine, / Their houses comfortable, / Their lives happy" (Laozi 2002: 83). The good life, why not? The point is not closing off the open through a system of rules and norms, but rather seeing the open as open and thereby doing something with it, or rather, in it. And the open is nothing but the meeting of mystery and simplicity, "a mixture of being and nothingness" (Bachelard 1964: 218); it is the simplest, yet the most elusive.

The concept of the glocal is well understood in Bachelard's elaboration on the relationship between the house and the world (or universe) in *The Poetics of Space*. This is not the same as the opposition between the closed and the open, for the house, *home*, becomes *a world, closed and open at the same time*, and in this sense it is the same as the concept of singularity, and one in which there is contamination. Bachelard quotes the poet Jules Supervielle on the capture of the outside and the paradox of 'too much freedom' as he rides the seemingly endless South American pampas, "Precisely because of too much riding and too much freedom, and of the unchanging horizon, in spite of our desperate gallopings, the pampa assumed the aspect of a prison for me, a prison that was bigger than the others" (221). Bachelard says that the phenomenology of the poetic imagination yields a notion of the human as a being that belongs to a borderline situation, a twilight, which he calls a "*surface*, the surface that separates the region of the same from the region of the other" (222); thus, a threshold. This is similar to the notion of "*being* a border oneself," rather than simply living "*on* a border," which Balibar mentions with a reference to the psychoanalyst André Green (Balibar 2002: 83). For Bachelard, the human being is "half-open being" (222). We still need to keep in mind Chapter Eighty of the *Daodejing*, to which we will soon return. I say this because, as we will see, there too we find the half-open condition and the becoming-a-border (in the sense of Deleuze and Guattari's becoming-x) of the human being; and this is true of the self as it is of the community. It is in other words, another instance of trans-dividuality. This twilight zone, this passage or threshold, this site of impermanence and vacillation, is the door, which, for Bachelard, is "an entire cosmos of the Half-open" (*ibid.*). The door, just like the border, divides and unites at the same time, or rather it is the neither/nor of unity and division. Yet, "there are two 'beings' in a door" (*ibid.*), just like at any border or threshold, and it is here again that we see the unsurpassable reality of trans-dividuality. And yet, a state of impermanence is better than one of finality, according to Bachelard (61), for this is where the imagination dwells, namely the possibility of rethinking and reshaping the world. Thus, as we will also see with Nishida in the last chapter of this book, it is not only a spatial threshold, but a temporal one as well: between the no-longer of the past and the not-yet of the future, hence one of projectuality. Inhabiting the same place and time once and forever is not possible; remaining the same is not possible, and the self is constantly expelled from itself, or rather it finds itself as constantly transgressing, constantly contaminated. Yet, the dream remains of settling somewhere, a dream that never ends. Bachelard says, "Housed everywhere but nowhere shut in, this is the motto of the dreamer of dwellings. In the last house as well as in the actual house, the day-dream of inhabiting is thwarted. A daydream of elsewhere should be left open therefore, at all times" (62). Singularity, however, is not simply a threshold, but rather the multiplicity of relations gathering at the threshold – each relation itself a threshold, and thus the site of a further gathering of multiple relations.

The last three lines of Chapter Eighty of the *Daodejing* describe this threshold and the problematic nature of dwelling and relating to one another. "Then even though neighboring states are within sight of each other, / Even though they can hear the sounds of each other's dogs and chickens, / Their people will grow old and die without ever having visited one another" (Laozi 2002: 83). As some commentators have noted, this might seem to be a conservative closure to the *Daodejing*. Others, however, have pointed out the potentially utopian dimension of these lines. What is clear is that the border, threshold, or door, what divides and unites at the same time, becomes a new singularity, maintaining itself in a metastable state. Interestingly, these lines do not say that there is no relationship whatsoever among neighbors. There is seeing and hearing; yet, there is no visiting – where visiting can also bring about conflict and includes modalities of violence. It would of course be implausible to think of this as an ante litteram description of virtual reality. Yet, at the same time, there is here an anticipation of Marramao's idea of a *universalism of difference*, of the unproblematic nature of the singular and common, and even of what, with a reference to Marx, we call the *general intellect*. In the context of Laozi's book, it is a utopia, or perhaps a heterotopia, in the sense that it is a correction of the dystopic modality brought about by doing too much, by becoming obsessed with accumulation and property, with discipline and order. Growing old and dying without going too far (without visiting one another) means being able to find the *Dao*, the way, anywhere – even within the innumerable folds of one's own self. This certainly relates to Chapter Forty-seven of the *Daodejing* where we read, "Without going out the door, one can know the whole world / . . . / The farther one goes, the less one knows," and this is why nonaction, *wu wei*, the doing of not doing is recommended. Just like in the passage by Supervielle about the never-ending pampa, quoted by Bachelard, the open (as potentiality) is not the mere outside (which might turn out to be the strongest prison), but rather the threshold, the door, the border, the half-open, which is an immanent crossing. It is often not the farthest, but perhaps the nearest, and it is usually not what is there, but what is not there.

The utopian, or heterotopic, character of the penultimate chapter of the *Daodejing*, where mystery and simplicity coincide, can be understood as a form of *poetic reverie*, in Bachelard's sense of the term, and truly as "an ontology of tranquility" (Bachelard 1971: 174). Bachelard addresses the phenomenological difference between a dream and a reverie (or daydream) in *The Poetics of Reverie* (1971). The poetic reverie, which is "a cosmic reverie," is "*an opening* to a beautiful world, to beautiful worlds" (13; emphasis added). What distinguishes it from the night dream, from a phenomenological point of view, is "the possible intervention of consciousness" (11). To use Paul Ricoeur's language, it is the fact of *attention*, its phenomenology, which is really the fact of freedom (2016: 41). However, this phenomenon does not present itself as the affirmation of a stable and unchanging self. Rather, as Bachelard says, it "gives the I a non-I which belongs to the I: my non-I" (13). It is again the gathering of a multiplicity of relations at the threshold, the neighboring spaces where there is virtual seeing and hearing, yet no displacing and conquering. In fact, a society dissolves as it becomes a world (14), many worlds (a world which includes many worlds, as the Zapatistas say). There is here ontological potency of a poetic (*poietic*) type, the creation – as Bachelard says following "Shelley and poets in general" (13–14) of an imaginary world, which absorbs within itself the real world in order to reshape it. It is in this sense that, Bachelard says, "the phenomenology of perception itself must stand aside for the phenomenology of the creative imagination" (14). What is brought about is, again, *an ontology of tranquility*, the multiplicity of thresholds and worlds, and, again, a universalism of difference.

In one of his greatest works, *Hölderlin's Hymn "The Ister,"* in the context of his explication of the essence of the *polis*, Martin Heidegger addresses the question of the open, which he treats in other works as well. The open is the singular, and it must be understood, for Heidegger, in relation to the meaning of *alētheia*, the disclosure of beings. Heidegger says that "seeing" the open, understood as disclosure, is "the distinction of human beings" (1996a: 91). He continues, "The animal is animal precisely on account of its not seeing the open, as understood in this way" (*ibid.*). Perhaps the easiest thing would be to say that there is anthropocentrism in this. However, this would be too hasty and ultimately superficial. Heidegger is here addressing the distinction, the essential difference, of the human animal, the human life-form, not its primacy in a hierarchical order of things. Thus, the repetition of the way in which we should understand the open here is all-important. Beings in general are in the open: "As unconcealed, beings are in the open" (*ibid.*). However, for Heidegger, seeing and naming, in the sense of "the 'is' or being," remain a human distinction. The strange or mysterious, the unhomely and uncanny, the unfamiliar, the "human abode in the midst of being," (*ibid.*) is the stage from which human beings undertake "the risk of becoming homely" (90). However, the difficulty is found in "the fact that the homely refuses itself to them" (*ibid.*). The human distinction is then that of a paradoxical condition. On the one hand, we see here the issue of the need to go from bare life to a type of life which is no longer bare (known as the good life), an issue to which we will go back; on the other hand, but in a closely related way, we see the idea, common in the tradition of philosophical anthropology, of a distinctive human deficiency or lack, especially in relation to the need of tools. This is also what brings to the fore, for Heidegger as well as others, the question of technology and of the transformation of what is 'given' in the first place, nature, understood by Heidegger as *phusis*, that which arises by itself. Indeed, in *The Question Concerning Technology*, showing the intimate relation between *phusis*, *poiēsis*, *technē*, and art, Heidegger describes the paradoxical condition of the human distinction, its standing in the open, as the twilight threshold of the familiar and the unfamiliar. First of all, Heidegger says, "*Physis* [*phusis*] also, the arising of something from out of itself, is a bringing-forth, *poiēsis*" (1977:10; brackets added). Then, we learn that *technē* also "belongs to bringing-forth, to *poiēsis*; it is something poietic" (13). And finally, we read that technology is only one form of *technē*: "Once there was a time when the bringing-forth of the true into the beautiful was called *technē*. And the *poiēsis* of the fine arts also was called *technē*" (34). Thus *phusis*, the self-arising, is *poiēsis*, bringing-forth, and *technē* and art are also forms of *poiēsis*. Moreover, art is, precisely, a form of *technē*. All this belongs in what we are here calling the ontology of unrest. The problem with Heidegger's thinking is that it apparently leads into a kind of fatalism. An instance of that is the idea of the pre-political and that "something has already been decided" (1996a: 9). Yet, in relation to the problematic nature of the open, there is much to learn, much to ponder. And the problematic nature of the open goes back to the idea of the half-open we have seen in Bachelard. This half-open is the same as Heidegger's idea of *revealing*, for we know that for Heidegger something remains concealed in unconcealment. He tells us that technology is also a revealing (1977: 14). Yet, (modern) technology is not a mere matter of human doing (19). Indeed, "man does not have control over unconcealment itself, in which at any given time the real shows itself or withdraws" (18). It is here that the question of the *danger*, so central in Heidegger's thought, becomes important. The danger is understood through the concept of Enframing (*Ge-stell*). This is so because Enframing contains and reveals the essence of modern technology. We can understand Enframing as a form of capture, thus a form of violence, in which something reveals and withdraws itself at the same time. But we are back to Heidegger's fatalism when he says that "Enframing is an ordaining destining" (24), in a way that recalls a line from Anaximander when he says ("in rather poetical language," according to Simplicius) that necessity works "in accordance with the ordering of time" (Curd 2011: 17).[3] Thus, "The essence of modern technology lies in Enframing. Enframing belongs within the destining of revealing" (25). To be sure, Heidegger himself tries to disambiguate this by saying that it has nothing to do with the usual notion of fate as "the inevitableness of an unalterable course" (*ibid.*). Fate is supposedly avoided precisely through and because of the singularity of the open, or, as Heidegger says, "that which is free – the mystery – [which] is concealed and always concealing itself" (*ibid.*). Thus, destiny or fate, Parmenides' *Moira*, has nothing to do with predestination, but rather with the permanence and constant sharing of what-is. Yet, what-is, in Heidegger's understanding of the closeness between Parmenides and Heraclitus, is in a constant state of agitation and unrest. For Heidegger, the danger, and indeed, "the supreme danger" (26), lies in the fact that Enframing blocks the open, conceals the revealing, and in so doing asserts itself and "reigns"(28) as the most disastrous event of capture. Thus, we find the famous statement, "What is dangerous is not technology" (*ibid.*). Rather, the danger is the essence of technology, "as a destining of revealing" (*ibid.*). We will deal again with the question of capture in a later chapter. For now, what is important is to highlight once again the paradox of the open. As framed singularity, the open ceases to be the open as such – or the multiplicity of its beings could not be seen or named – and it becomes the site of the gathering of that multiplicity of relations, a threshold, as we have seen. There is *poiēsis* (production), and yet *poiēsis* is blocked. The question, perhaps, is to interrogate the nature of this destining, or direction, the nature of Enframing, or framing, which in the age of digital technology and the General Intellect does not become less uncanny.

Enframing is a form of capture. For humans, this capture takes on the form of what Arnold Gehlen calls "the *circle of action*" (1980: 17), which ultimately develops into a set of automatisms. I will go back to Gehlen's analysis in a later chapter. For now, I will only note that these automatisms are linked to the human power to act and to the original "enigma" (4), "mysterious law" (6) or "magic" (12, 17), which for Gehlen define the nature more than the condition of the human being, or perhaps something which is between nature and condition. Thus, as Gehlen says, "man himself *is* an automatism" (15), and this makes up for the original, "organic and instinctual deficiencies" of human beings (4). This original deficiency and lack of specialization is another way of addressing the question of the open; the human as "world-open" (Gehlen 1988: 27). The non-human animal, on the other hand, is, according to Giorgio Agamben, "closed in the circle of its disinhibitors" (2004: 51), and with a reference to Jacob von Uexküll, he continues, "closed in the few elements that define its perceptual world" (*ibid.*). Agamben highlights the "relationship between the animal's 'poverty in world' (*Weltarmut*) and 'world-forming' (*weltbilden*) man" (50) articulated by Heidegger. Perhaps there is capture in both conditions. Yet, the framing proper of *technē*, and thus of *poiēsis* (though blocked), the capture at the threshold of the half-open, seems to characterize the condition of the human more than that of the non-human animal. As Agamben says, the ontological difference lies in the fact that the environment of the non-human animal is *open* (and indeed fully open), but not *openable*, or *disconcealed*, that is, half-open. He says, "This *openness without disconcealment* distinguishes the animal's poverty in world from the world-forming which characterizes man" (55). Thus, only the human animal "can see the open which names the unconcealedness of beings. The [non-human] animal, on the contrary, never sees the open" (58; brackets added). The epigraph for this chapter of Agamben's book *The Open* is Heidegger's statement, "Not even the lark sees the open" (57), and the reason for this is that the lark is *fully* in the open. Thus, although there is capture in both conditions, Enframing, the framing of *technē*, with its injunction to a blocked *poiēsis* (and a difficult *praxis*), constitutes a remarkable complication, which usually goes under the name of freedom.

Thus, Agamben says, "The animal environment is constituted in such a way that something like a pure possibility can never become manifest within it" (68). It is an environment which is "neither-open-nor-closed" (*ibid.*), a neither/nor situation which is different from the half-open one of the human being we have seen in Bachelard. Perhaps there is no mystery, or magic, but full simplicity in the environment of the non-human animal, the full simplicity of being there, without the complication of freedom or boredom (63–70). This is so because the very fact that there may be a mystery comes to the fore only in the open ontology that discloses the end of simplicity and the difficult passage onto the plane of potentiality and the potentiality-not-to, that is to say, of contingency. This simplicity is perhaps suspended in the human condition, which is, Agamben says, "a suspension of animality" itself (73). This suspension is the threshold, or what Agamben calls the "between" (81-84). Here Agamben quotes Walter Benjamin who, in "One-Way Street," says, "And likewise technology is the mastery not of nature but mastery of the relation between nature and humanity" (83). Yet, the essence of *technē* is different from what appears at the threshold, in the half-open or "between" as the possibility of the formation of technology, which is equally the possibility inherent in poetry (*poiēsis*), art, and human action (*praxis*) in general. Speaking of Aristotle in his little book on the relationship between the human and non-human animal, Gilbert Simondon highlights the importance of "the functions of life" (2011: 52). We know how important the concept of function or work (*ergon*) is for Aristotle. In Book I of his *Ethics*, he says that in order to know what human life is we have first to determine what the human function is. This turns out to be "activity of the psyche in accordance with reason, or excellence (virtue)" (1999: 1098a 5–20; translation modified). Yet, everything has a function, and despite the changes due to different individuations, "the function remains" (Simondon 2011: 51). Simondon repeats this phrase a few times in his pages on Aristotle. He says, "What is not possible with certain faculties can be achieved by others and the functions remain" (*ibid.*). More importantly, beyond the specificity of any form of individuation, "there is an invariant, and this invariant is life; the functions of life; the means used to fulfill these functions change with species, but the functions remain, life in an invariant" (52). Perhaps we find in the end an even broader *universalism of difference*, a certain order, or harmony, as Leibniz, the thinker of contingency, says. But for Leibniz, who despite his idealist philosophy comes here close to the materialist positions of thinkers like Spinoza and Leopardi, this order includes what might appear to us as disorderly. Perhaps contingency is a moment of true, singular *dis*order, not in the sense that it brings about the disorderly and irregular, but in the sense that it raises the initial simplicity to the level of the mysterious; it shows "the crack in everything" (as Leonard Cohen has it), the open, the multitudinous gathering at the threshold. Obviously, contingency has nothing to do with free will, but with mystery. Lucretius' notion of *clinamen*, the unpredictable swerve of the atoms, is also a matter of contingency, *the necessity of contingency*, as in Louis Althusser's astonishing concept (Althusser and Balibar 1997: 45). What remains true, as Leibniz says, is that despite the hypothesis of order, it is not possible to explain "the great mystery upon which the entire universe depends" (1989: 39). But what Leibniz says is close to Spinoza's truth that reality and perfection are the same (1992: 152).

NOTES

1. There is a reference to Serge Latouche's book, *The Westernization of the World*.
2. The translation of passages from Miquel (2019) is my own.
3. We will go back to Heidegger's reading of the Anaximander fragment in a later chapter.

TWO

Replacing the Individual

The Impossible Individuation

In the Introduction to *L'individuation à la lumière des notions de forme et d'information*, Gilbert Simondon speaks of the idea of "replacing the individual" according to a theory that sees being, not as a stable and fixed category, but as a metastable and open process that goes from the preindividual to the transindividual, and, one might say, back into itself (2013: 32).[1] In Simondon's work, the individual is exploded, or it can be exploded, eliminated, or surpassed. The individual is not replaced by the transindividual, or by a relapse into a preindividual reality. Rather, the individual becomes a true impossibility insofar as individuation as such, that is, as a complete result of the individuating process, is also impossible. To say that individuation is impossible does not imply that there is no ongoing process of individuation, but simply that there is no result (no end) to such a process. The process itself remains open, an asymptotic movement, an infinite expansion. Perhaps there is the semblance of a closure in physical individuation (in the crystal, as in Simondon's paradigmatic case) – but there, too, perhaps only a semblance. Yet, in what Simondon calls vital (biological) and then, psychic and, especially, collective individuation (transindividuation), there is no such a closure at all. All there is are fragments in search of individuation, constantly individuating, yet regularly falling short of full individuation. It is in this sense that to the concept of the individual I prefer the concept of the dividual (or rather, the gathering of dividuals), and to transindividuation, transdividuation. Indeed, as Nietzsche says, the individual is "the most recent creation" (1978: 59). Obviously, the extremely common concept of the individual has some transitional usefulness and importance, and so does the much less known (indeed almost unknown) concept of the transindividual. In a manner similar to Spinoza's remark on the usefulness of (or the need to retain) concepts such as good and bad – though they are only *modes of thinking* (Spinoza 1992: 153) – we can say that the concept of the individual must be retained until society, and indeed the world, is ready for the true meaning of the singular. Yet, this must be a preparatory and critical time. During this time, the concept of the individual must be under a regime of constant critique, under attack; it must be fully deconstructed and ultimately done with. Simondon speaks of the *relative individual* (2013: 25) and of a *theater* of individuation (27). All this points to the unnecessary and, really, false negation of the dividual in the 'in- (the not)' of the individual. This negation is neither dialectical nor *transductive* in Simondon's sense of the word (i.e., the sense proper to individuation; I will say more about this below). In fact, what is technically a negation regularly appears as a wholly positive reality and an irrefutable truth. The transition is then easily made to the independent and sovereign individual, the cause of so much damage and sorrow.

It is clear that for Simondon impossible are both the individual as a stable and absolute entity and the accomplished, closed and total, individuation. Indeed, when Simondon says "relative individual," he denies the individual altogether, for the latter is regularly understood as a simple, unified, and absolute reality. The individual does not exist, either as a principle or as a result of the process of individuation. To be sure, Simondon does not explicitly deny the existence of the individual. For instance, he sees becoming as a constitutive relation of being qua individual: "*becoming is not opposed to being; it is the constitutive relation of being as an individual*" (91; original emphasis). He also says, "The individual is *being and relation*; it is the center of activity, but this activity is transductive" (143; original emphasis). Yet, this says that we are not dealing with the concept of the individual in its common usage. Rather, the individual here is *a theater* in the dephasing (*déphasage*) of being, in its open unfolding. This really means that the same problem that applies, for Simondon, to the concept of principle in 'principle of individuation' (23) also applies to individuation itself. Simondon challenges the idea that individuation has a principle, for "[i]n this very notion of principle, there is a certain character that prefigures the constituted individuality, with the property that it will have once it is constituted" (*ibid.*). Paolo Virno points out that John Duns Scotus also challenged the idea of the principle of individuation. For Virno, both Scotus and Simondon "contested the usual way of understanding the *principium individuationis* and above all its reduction to a localised question without true consequences for general ontology" (Virno 2009: 59). The localized question would be to ascribe to a particular aspect of reality the capacity to guarantee "the singularity of an entity" (60). To the contrary, Virno stresses the preindividual reality of the *common*, "deprived of numerical unity" (*ibid.*) and structuring the singular. Indeed, it is the singular, the multiplicity of singularities, not the constituted or individuated individuals, which unfold from the common and return to it. Yet, the common, "inferior to numerical unity" for Duns Scotus (see Virno 2009: 61), preindividual for Simondon, is not at all a principle. Thus, there is no *principle* of individuation. However, as I have noted above, the same applies to individuation as such, for the constituted, stable individuality would deny the principles of metastability and transduction (the structuring operation of individuation), whereby the real (rich with potentialities) constantly unfolds. There is then no individuation in the sense of the coming to completion of the individuating process; rather, there is only constant individuating. This individuating process does not even end with death, for there is at death, and after death, decomposition and a return. Indeed, as Bernard Stiegler says, "Death itself is such an incompletion" (2009: 55). The important point to be grasped is that there is no individuation behind or past individuating; thus individuation is not even a result of the individuating process. This process remains open one way or another, or truly in a multiplicity of ways. The point is then to create the conditions whereby the singular can appear as singular. But the singular is always an individuating plurality, *a more and less than unity and identity*, as Simondon often says (2013: e.g., 26, 29). The individual, and thus individuation, is a relative reality. The process of individuation, as Virno says, "is always circumscribed and partial – indeed unfinishable by definition" (2009: 64). The individual as a *relative reality* presupposes, for Simondon, a preindividual reality (the common for Virno), but "even after individuation, it does not exist just by itself, for individuation does not exhaust in just one time the potentialities of preindividual reality" (Simondon 2013: 24–25). Simondon also says that the relativity of the individual is twofold. The individual is relative "because it is not the whole of being and because it is the result of a state of being in which it did not exist either as individual or as principle of individuation" (25).

Thus, the difference between the individual and the singular is not that the singular is something beyond, or more (or less) than, the individual. It is rather completely different from it. It is not its excess or surplus. Rather, the singular is a trans-conceptual reality, the common, a concrete abstraction, a measureless and potential thisness each time contracted and actualized in every *this*; it is the infinitizing mode of every finitude, an exit or escape, and, finally, the *transductive* (more than dialectical) negation of the dividual. To say that it is transductive means to say that what defines it is the *tension* (Simondon 2013: 33) present throughout the *dephasing of being* (*déphasage de l'être*), its metastable unfolding from the preindividual, which is, however, especially in the case of the living being, never exhausted in the collective and trans-dividual infinitizing moment. For Virno, "singularity emerges from the preliminary sharing of a preindividual reality: X and Y are individuated individuals only because they display what they have in common differently" (2009: 61). The individuated individual is truly the dividual, which draws its singularity by its attachment to the common and by expressing it. It expresses it in a way that is *problematic*, as Simondon repeatedly stresses. What is problematic is precisely the fact that, in the living being, the preindividual remains as permanent potential, as becoming (Simondon 2013: 29); the turbulence of the common is carried within the singular. In the case of psychic individuation, this problematic fact also gives rise to what Simondon calls the *internal resonance* (*la résonance interne*), which is another name for singularity, or what really constitutes singularity's structure, or schematism, or aura. I will go back to this in the final chapter of this book. The singular, completely different from the individual, is not beyond the common, outside it. Rather, in expressing the common through difference, without ever becoming identical with itself, it turns out to be the threshold of the common, the half-open, or, as in Simondon's wonderful metaphor, a *theater of individuation*, namely, the theater of the unfolding of the common, the dephasing of being. What we also see here is that this potency of permanent unfolding and becoming, this open-ended process is, paradoxically, a constraint. This is what Paul-Antoine Miquel says speaking about life and the biosphere: there is "a constraint of permanent opening" ["*une contrainte de permanente ouverture*"] (2019: 59). Furthermore, this "constraint of opening is open on itself!" (*ibid.*), and this means that such potency is "permanence deprived of itself, late to its identity" (*ibid.*). It is like opening up Parmenides' apparently closed sphere of being, its fullness, absolutely identical with itself. Yet, this also, once again, indicates the ultimately impossible individuation and the truth that the individuating process remains open. Miquel speaks of this as of a "totality open on itself and yet less than itself." He also says that "its identity . . . never stops redefining and recomposing itself" (60). It is the "potency of permanent recomposition" ["*un potential de permanent recomposition*"], which he calls plasticity, *plasticité* (*ibid.*). Plasticity means that "a system has the potential to never keep itself as it is" (63). Thus the *recomposition* is such that there is always a *delay* of "the conditions of its individuation" (*ibid.*). Miquel uses here the notions of subtraction and dissipation, whereby there is always a structural incompletion and a permanent heterogeneity. He is here speaking about the biosphere and about Venus, one of the characters of his *philo fiction*, as he describes his narrative, of which, he says, Simondon was one of the initiators (41). However, he bases his argument on Simondon's metaphor of the living being as not only an agent but a *theater* of individuation. In this sense, his argument can be generalized to all individuation. Essentially, the implication is that identity is unachievable and that individuation is impossible. Perhaps there is virtual or potential identity, but "it is never fully actualized, individuated" (*ibid.*). In addition to the importance of this for an understanding of any individuating process, we might remark on the fact that this theory runs counter to the often-made claim that there is, in ontology, no reserve of becoming or potency and that therefore all that can be must be actual. Miquel says the opposite: never fully actualized, the potential remains as potential because of a movement of self-subtraction, a delay, and a dissipative tension, in which "there is a construction within destruction" (62). This is the "potential of permanent plasticity" (63), the preindividual, to use Simondon's language, which grounds the singular as thisness without number, relations without a subject.

The relationship between the common and the singular can also be understood in terms of plasticity. Indeed, as Virno says, their relationship is similar to the one between potentiality and actuality. He says, "The Singular is not distinguished from the Common for possessing some supplementary quality but because it determines in a contingent and unrepeatable manner all the qualities already included in it" (2009: 63). Thus, he speaks of "a *modal* individuation" (*ibid.*; original emphasis), namely, "the passage from one mode of being to another" (*ibid.*), and he attributes this to the thought of both Duns Scotus and Simondon. This plasticity of being, this transductive and modal passage from the common to the singular, to the many singularities gathering at the threshold, and then back to the common, is precisely what the never-ending process of individuation truly is. In fact, individuation does not happen all at once, and ultimately, in the sense of a closure, it does not happen at all, but the individuating process permanently goes on. We have already seen how Virno calls this process "unfinishable by definition" (64). He then highlights the importance of the preposition *between*,[2] which, "usually employed carelessly, is the best that ordinary language provides to indicate that which, while really existing outside the mind, is nonetheless 'inferior to numerical unity'" (*ibid.*). Virno is speaking in terms of politics and political ontology. He says that the "'between' designates the sphere of productive cooperation and political conflict" (*ibid.*). Indeed, without the between what may appear as individuals would be fragments, mere dividuals. For Virno, it is the common that shows itself in the 'between,' not only now as preindividual, but also as transindividual. He calls it "the public sphere of the multitude" (*ibid.*). My thesis is that it is really a matter of trans-dividuality. The otherwise unrelated fragments, which, contrary to all appearance, never attain full individuality, gather at the threshold, the 'between,' the half-open of the commonality of the singular and the singularity of the common. They become not relational individuals, but relational singularities. They become networks of cooperation, assemblages. The fact that we have the appearance of the individuals should not deceive us. The main question in Jason Read's book on the politics of transindividuality is precisely that of the effacement of the conditions of transindividuality in the appearance of the sovereign and independent individual (Read 2016). To go back to some of Miquel's notions seen above, the fact remains that the singular is the common *in subtraction of itself*, just as the common is *the potency of permanent plasticity*. Ultimately, the singular and the common are the same, as Virno stresses, the former expressing the latter each time in a different way. But the singular should not be understood as another word for the individual, which, as we have seen, does not exist. The singular is the gathering of commonalities expressed in fragments, dividuals and differences; the gathering gives rise to the collective, the assemblage and network. As Virno points out, for Simondon "the collective does not attenuate singularity, but sharpens and strengthens it" (2009: 65). Indeed, without the collective, which is the most singular expression of the common, there would only be unrelated fragments, scattered and wholly disindividuated. These fragments constitute what in modernity we usually refer to as individuals.

To deny the individual and even individuation as a completed process does not at all alter the importance of the process itself. Simondon speaks of various phases of individuations: physical, psychic, and collective. However, the central moment in all this is the dynamic trajectory traced by *transduction*, which is a "structuring operation" and "an individuation in progress" (Simondon 2013: 33). Even when we consider what might seem to be the last stage of dephasing and of structuring transduction, namely, collective individuation, or rather "the systematic unity of interior (psychic) individuation and exterior (collective) individuation" (29), we realize that precisely that is not the end of all, that is to say, it is not the arrival to a closed situation. Indeed, this *is* the transindividual. The individual becomes a group individual, not in the sense of the interindividual, but of the transindividual (*ibid.*). But the transindividual presents itself as a new opening, or rather as the open potency of the preindividual that has not been exhausted and cannot be exhausted. Distinguishing between the interindividual and transidividual relations, Simondon says that the former "goes from individual to individual," and he adds that "it does not penetrate the individuals" (294). The latter, however, is "the action ... that makes it possible for individuals to exist together as elements of a system with potential and metastability, expectation and tension" (*ibid.*). He also says, "The transindividual goes on in the individual just as it does from individual to individual" (*ibid.*). Thus, the transindividual includes the modality of interindividuality, but it adds the moment or structure of penetration, which is what I call 'the gathering.' Fundamentally, however, the transindividual action "does not localize the individuals" (*ibid.*); the structuring transduction and the penetrating gathering remain unresolved, open. This is true at the inner (psychic) level and at the outer (collective) level. It is in this sense that I prefer to stress the fact that the individual never obtains as such, never is finalized, and the process of transindividuation is truly one of transdividuation. The reality that, Simondon says, "can be named transindividual" (295) is ontologically constituted by the preindividual, which remains there as open potential. Simondon says that such reality "has neither a social nor an individual origin." Instead, "it is deposited in the individual, carried by it, but it does not belong to it or become part of its system of being as an individual" (*ibid.*). Let me stress again that Simondon says that this reality *can be* called transindividual. This leaves open the question of the adequacy of its name, and again that is not at all a question of terminology. What is important is the potency carried within what appears as an individuated being, the "charge of being (*charge d'être*) for future individuations" (*ibid.*). Simondon says, "The individual is not simply individual, but also *reserve of being* still unpolarized, available, waiting" (*ibid.*). In fact, the individual is not all an individual, but a dividual (or a bundle of dividuals) waiting for the (inner and outer) gathering, *in search of the singular*.[3] Indeed, what the structuring operation of transduction brings about is not individuation, but singularization.

The singular is precisely the "particular being" that is "more than an individual" (301). I will go back to this in the next chapter, on the question of the subject. For now, I want to point out that for Simondon individuation is "a phase of being" (*une phase de l'être*; *ibid.*). Again, the most important element in all this is that the preindividual is not exhausted in the process of individuation, but it remains there as potency. In this sense, Simondon's discourse on transindividuality is truly about preindividuality, which, as a non-numeric reality, informs all phases of being. In fact, transindividuality is a little too close to interindividuality. To me, what really count here are the preindividual and the structuring operation of transduction. In and through these, we have the immanent passage from the common to the singular, the common remaining within the singular, the singular experiencing and expressing the common in its own way, producing the threshold where the gathering happens. This is also what signification and communication are about. It is not a question of "form informing matter" (304), such as it is in the hylemorphic paradigm; it is rather the ontogenetic unfolding through *transduction*, which, Simondon says, "grounds being in an absolute manner" (*ibid.*). It is as if Simondon were here describing Parmenides' sphere crossed through and shaken, burst open, by Heraclitus' metastable flow of becoming. Simondon's critique of the hylemorphic paradigm essentially points out the existence in that paradigm of "an obscure zone" (303), which "prevents the knowledge of *ontogenesis*" (*ibid.*) and thus of "the central operational zone" of transindividuation, namely, transduction. At the level of psychic and collective individuation, that is to say, the individuation of living beings, or transindividuality, the never-exhausted preindividual potency manifests itself as *emotion*. Simondon says that "emotion is the preindividual manifested within the subject" (305). It is not of the individual as an individuated being. Rather, within the subject, it is "an exchange between the preindividual and the individuated being" (*ibid.*), which is what I call the dividual. Moreover, it "prefigures the discovery of the collective" (*ibid.*). This is really what happens at the threshold of singularization.

It is not the case that the preindividual is first in a chronological sense. In other words, there is not a linear passage from the preindividual to the individual and then to the transindividual. Rather, the preindividual endures as an ontological, or ontogenetic, power throughout the individuating process, the structuring operation of transduction. The individuating process, as we have seen, never ends, and individuation as a closed result, namely, the individual, never truly obtains. This is the result of Simondon's approach, which is that of "knowing the individual through individuation rather than individuation starting from the individual" (24); the latter approach is the one that makes use of the notion of a principle of individuation. Thus the relative individual both exists and does not exist. However, the absolute individual as a permanent phase of being does not exist at all. What is permanent, in fact, is the potency of the preindividual, which is *being without phases* (25). It is through *becoming*, an aspect of being (*dimension de l'être*), that the individuating process, the dephasing of being unfolds. Indeed, this individuating process is becoming itself. As Simondon says, individuation is not at all "a consequence deposed at the edge of becoming and isolated" (*ibid.*). It is the individuating process itself, not its consequence; or rather, as I prefer to say, the trans-dividuating process. In fact, what appears in the dephasing or unfolding of being is the individual and its environment, the *individual-milieu couple*, which for Stiegler (2007: 48) resonates with the Heideggerian being-in-the-world, and thus (perhaps even more so), we may add, with the notion of being-with, where collective in-dividuation is more clearly represented. It is thus the relative individual, or the network of dividuals, the gathering at the threshold. This network of dividuals is the relations without a subject that we will see again later. Relations, or structures, are the contingent and transient effect of the resolution of tensions brought about by becoming. The tensions belong in the preindividual, which is "more than a unit" (*ibid.*), namely, more than an individual being, more than identity. However, these tensions remain present in the domain of the living being, where, in addition to the individual/environment duality, one also finds "a permanent activity of individuation" (27). It is here that we find the first occurrence of the expression *theater of individuation*. Simondon says that the living being "is not simply the result of individuation, like the crystal or the molecule, but a theater of individuation" (*ibid.*), that is, an open gathering, an impossible closure, and trans-dividuation. For him, this is the metastable condition of life (28), which intimately relates to the *internal resonance*, "which requires a permanent communication" (27). However, it seems to me that the network of relations, if not the theater of individuation, is also found in physical individuation, not only in the domain of the living being. In fact, even in the former what counts is the process, not its result or consequence. To be sure, for Simondon the difference lies in the concept of *the limit* (29). Both individuations have internal resonance, but the domain of the living being also features a "veritable interiority," which the physical individual lacks. Thus, "the living being is within itself a node of informative communication; it is a system within a system" (28). However, as we will see, the advance of digital technology may well complicate this in the sense that perhaps this interiority becomes more superficial or is in excess of itself, a kind of amplification, as it would be in the case of machinic assemblage. But this is in fact the external relation that for Simondon signals the passage from psychic to collective individuation, and thus to transindividuality. The notion of 'veritable interiority' is what we will call the schematism, or personality, within singularity at the end of the book.

Excess relates to the inexhaustible potency of the preindividual, and this is, once again, what gives the individual only a *relative* reality. Indeed, "a certain level of potential remains, and individuations are still possible" (*ibid.*). To say that the preindividual is not exhausted means that it is carried within the individual itself, it remains *associated* with it. This is the same as saying that the individual is not fully an individual. It remains in a state of metastability from which new individuations may arise. This is what gives the living being (or any individuated entity, for that matter) its problematic nature, of being, for instance, "at the same time more and less than a unit" (29). Simondon says that the problematic nature of the living being is "broader [*plus vaste*] than its own being" (*ibid.*), and this is the path into the transindividual, which is mentioned here in the introduction for the first time. This path is necessarily transductive. Transduction is the central moment, or relation, in the process of individuation. It is a structuring and molecular operation. Indeed, it is "an individuation in progress" (33), which "retains all the concrete" (34), and thus is the singular as such. But, contrary to a reduction to the individual and the one, what we have here is a plurality of possible individuations and thus of singularities. In this sense, Simondon says, we should also consider the existence of "several logics, each corresponding to a definite type of individuation" (36). To speak about "pluralizing logic" (*pluraliser la logic*) (*ibid.*) means to individuate a mode of communication, truly, the common, whereby singularities can appear and endure as singularities. In a very Parmenidean move, necessary to accompany the very Heraclitean phenomenon of transduction, Simondon says that "only the individuation of thought can, in accomplishing itself, accompany the individuation of beings other than thought" (*ibid.*). I am of course thinking of Parmenides' fragments, "for the same thing is for thinking and for being" (Curd 2011: 58) and "What is for thinking is the same as that on account of which there is thought" (60). This "parallel operation" (Simondon 2013: 36) is also in line with Spinoza's thought about the parallel structure of thought and extension, the two attributes of substance (one substance, but a one which is not a numeric unit) known to us. Transduction is, however, a phenomenological mode of unfolding (and a mode of communication) whereby individuation cannot really be known, not "in the habitual sense of the term" (*ibid.*), but rather it becomes a matter of self-enveloping, an inner and outer individuation, which is really a trans-dividuation.

It is in Stiegler that we find some basis for a theory of trans-dividuation. Indeed, especially when it comes to individuating the present, where we experience de-individuation and disindividuation, trans-dividuation becomes apparent. What Stiegler calls "the *whats [les quois]*" (2009: 48), which is the *milieu* for Simondon (in the *individual-milieu couple*), becomes the basis for trans-dividuation, especially in the digital age. The individual, even when there is such a one, is always *with the whats*. To be sure, Simondon does not explicitly deny the existence of the individual, though, as we have seen, the *relative* nature of the individual is most essential in his theory. And we know that for him transduction itself starts, for some reason, from a center of preindividual being. For Stiegler, however, transindividuation, as "the *essential fragility* of individuation" (2009: 51), is also *deindividuation* and *disindividuation*. In a sense, this is the danger, a loss of individuation, as well as a process of desingularization, "with singularity being that which must be reduced to particularity" (*ibid.*). This is precisely the danger of the politics of number. It is especially in relation to the machine that this process of disindividuation and desingularization becomes evident, and this is what, for Stiegler, changes the being-with of the 'we' to "the hegemony of the *they*" (52). His claim is that Heidegger speaks of the 'they,' namely, of the fall, and Simondon speaks of the 'we.' Addressing Heidegger's concept of *Dasein*, which is neither an 'I' nor a 'we,' but prior and indifferent to this distinction (48), Stiegler highlights the reality of disindividuation as a phenomenon of subjection to the 'they,' the neutral *who* to which even being-with has to yield. Stiegler's reference is to *Being and Time*, where Heidegger says, "The who is not this one and not that one, not oneself and not some and not the sum total of them all. The 'who' is the neuter, *the they*" (1996b: 118–119). Essentially, Heidegger is addressing what he calls "the *entanglement* of Dasein," which is not "a 'fall' from a purer and higher 'primordial condition'" (164). As *facticity*, which, Stiegler says does not concern Simondon at all, Dasein has, for Heidegger, "already fallen *away from itself*" (*ibid.*), namely, it has fallen prey. Heidegger also says, "Falling prey is an existential determination of Dasein" (*ibid.*), but it also "reveals an *essential*, ontological structure of Dasein itself" (168). Yet, this *who* that is *the they* is no *who* at all, for the *who*, especially in its neutrality, is ultimately impossible; or rather, as Antonio Negri says in a different context, the *who* is the same as the *how* (in Bobbio 1987: 131). This means that disindividuation, the loss of individuation, is not something that happens at one point in time, due, for instance, to the conditions of alienation in production and work, but it is always there. The preindividual itself is trans-dividual. It is not a question of choosing between the 'we' and the 'they,' nor is neutrality a matter of the 'who,' insofar as there is no subject. This does not mean that the singular, which regularly appears as an individual, an 'I,' is simply a part of a greater whole in a mechanical or machinic sense. It is rather an element *of* and *in* transduction, a structuring operation that always takes place in disindivinduation.

As Simondon says, "the individuated being is at the same time alone and not-alone" ["l'être individué est à la fois seul et non-seul"] (2013: 246). Perhaps we find here the distance between the 'we' and the 'they,' and certainly the meaning of disindividuation and trans-dividuation. The in-dividuated being is truly *unalone*, to use a wonderful expression by William Faulkner (1987: 56). To be unalone is precisely to be alone and not-alone at the same time. As Nancy Blake points out in her psychoanalytic and Lacanian analysis of Faulkner's *As I Lay Dying*, Faulkner's "invented negatives" are well known (1985: 562). As she says, "'Unalone' in the discourse of Dewey Dell," one of the characters in *As I Lay Dying*, "aims at the expression of a solitude at once violated and reinforced" (*ibid.*). For her, the "fragmentary monologues" that make up Faulkner's novel, say that "the subject is not the individual, but . . . the result of the experience of a speaker who can never know what he says" (*ibid.*). Indeed, "a text, or a discourse, or a body for that matter, does not belong to an individual" (560). The logic of trans-dividuality is implied by Blake in a rather strong way when she says that Faulkner's characters are "puppets set in motion by speech which is not their own" (555). The "polyphonic narration" (554), typical of Faulkner's novels, is here dominated by the dying, then dead, mother (*ibid.*). It is in this sense that, Blake says, the "I" in the title is not a subject, but a signifier: it "is everyone," or death itself as "a common denominator" (*ibid.*). This is also evident in the milieu, in the objects in the novel, the drawn image on the page of the coffin of the mother (559; Faulkner 1987: 77). Blake says, "Faulkner's text is not so much narration as re-present-ation" (1985: 559). It is the speech of death as the representation of death. It is the death of both the one and the other, the negation of individuality, and the discovery of the singular, the *unalone*. It is a transduction beyond the dialectic, that is to say, the negative that remains suspended in a metastable state of tension as dephasing of being, thus as preindividual, perhaps akin to the potentiality-not-to. I would say that it is the negation of the subject as well – though Blake in a sense already implies that by saying that the "I" is not a subject but a signifier, as we have seen, and by referring to Jacques Lacan's notion of the *knot*, "which ties presence to absence in the fullness of impossibility" (562). It is essentially a question of relations without a subject.

In order to see this better, we need to go back to the individual-milieu couple, where the dividual is more easily discernible. I would like to give an illustration of this by referring to Stanley Laurel and Oliver Hardy's movies, and in particular to *The Music Box* (1932). Like many other of their movies (for instance, *County Hospital* or *Another Fine Mess*), this is a perfect example of trans-dividuation and of the individual-milieu situation. The movie is about the impossible individuation and the end of the individual. Stan and Ollie are delivering a piano to a house which stands at the top of a public staircase in Los Angeles. They ask a postman for directions, and he shows them the house at the top of the staircase without telling them that there is also a road they can take to get there. This starts all kinds of disastrous situations typical of Laurel and Hardy's movies. In particular, there is an interesting interaction with the horse carrying the piano, which shows the continuity between human and non-human cunning intentionality; the argument with a woman with a baby carriage, which calls into question 'proper' gender relations, something Stan often does when he addresses a man of authority as 'ma'am'; the resulting fight with a policeman, to whom Stan says, "Don't you think you're bounding over your steps?" And Ollie comes to his rescue telling the police officer, "He means overstepping your bounds"; then, especially, the encounter with the German professor who turns out to be the owner of the house at the top of the steps. When he goes back home and sees what Stan and Ollie have done to his house, completely enraged he asks, "What is the meaning of this?" This is actually a key question that is at times asked by some characters in Laurel and Hardy's movies. The meaning of 'this' might be impossible individuation and impossible subjectivation, but it is certainly also the unwillingness to remain in a state of subjection, in one's own place as an individual, which is really what constitutes the *subversive* dimension of Laurel and Hardy's movies. What appears then is an ensemble of confused relations rather than a stable subject, or sovereign individual. There is no longer an individual-milieu couple, but a plurality of dividuals in an utterly destroyed milieu. Everything becomes metastable, and it endures as such. Perhaps it must be highlighted that this destructive moments in Laurel and Hardy's movies are never gratuitous, but rather they are the ground for new action and production, new constitution (or combination) of being, a transduction and a trans-stitution (or transposition). They are similar to a potlatch situation, namely, the destruction of the accursed share at all levels of the dephasing of being. This is to say that they are part of "the critique or deconstruction of interiority, of self-presence, of consciousness, of mastery, of the individual or collective property of an essence," as Jean-Luc Nancy says in the introduction to *Who Comes after the Subject?* (Cadava, Connor, and Nancy 1991: 4).

The apparent lack of mastery, the indiscipline we have seen in talking about Laurel and Hardy is really a powerful way of challenging the docility-utility intended by the implementation of a series of technics, which Foucault calls "disciplines" (1977: 137). It is the destruction of the individual and its place. Foucault says that disciplinary machinery does not simply work on the principle of "enclosure" (and thus confinement), but "first of all on the principle of elementary location or *partitioning*" (143). Accordingly, "Each individual has his own place; and each place its individual" (*ibid.*). To challenge this principle, which is easily carried from the disciplinary society to the society of surveillance and control, means to produce disorder and chaos, or what at first appears as such; what certainly appears as such from the viewpoint of the system of law and order. But the most important implication is that the place of the individual becomes a vortex and the individual is crushed within it, until, as in Zeno's paradox, the notion of place itself becomes inconceivable. Unchallenged, the principle of partitioning is perfected in the structure of the Panopticon (and today the digital system of surveillance, the virtual Panopticon), which "assures the automatic functioning of power" (201). From the point of view of the system, the multitude "is replaced by a multiplicity that can be numbered and supervised;" from the point of view of singularities, "by a sequestered and observed solitude" (*ibid.*). Obviously, Foucault's reference is to Jeremy Bentham's principle whereby power, to be most effective, must be visible and unverifiable. The Panopticon is "a machine for dissociating the see/being seen dyad" (201-202); as such, it "automatizes and disindividualizes power" (202). In the digital age, with the virtual Panopticon, the resulting subjection and disindividuation, while preserving the illusion of freedom, not only produce, but "train or correct individuals" (203) even outside of the prison walls, or those of any total institution. Of course, it is one of Foucault's main theses that in modernity the prison is extended to society as a whole. Indeed, society becomes the *laboratory* that the Panopticon was (*ibid.*). Thus, we live under the injunction to become individuals, occupy our place, and forget the preindividual potency, that ontological force, which constantly throws us back into the metastable process for which there is no closure. This individuality, a "real subjection" (202), is nothing but dividuation and disindividuation, and it conceals the tumultuous gathering at the threshold, the trans-dividual. In the next chapter, we will see the implications of dividuation for a critical theory of the subject and subjectivity.

NOTES

1. *L'individuation à la lumière des notions de forme et d'information*, Simondon's doctoral thesis of 1958, was published in its entirety in France only in 2005. Here I use the 2013 edition. The thesis (and thus the book) is divided into two parts: *L'individuation physique* (Physical Individuation) and *L'individuation des etrês vivants* (The Individuation of Living Beings). The second part contains the chapters on psychic and collective individuation, and thus on transindividuality. All quotes from this book are my translation.
2. In this sense, see also Jean-Luc Nancy (2000).
3. I owe the expression "in search of the singular" to Michael Pelias.

THREE

Subject of Fiction

Subjection and Subjugation

All theory of the subject and subjectivity must ultimately be a theory of subjection (and, as we will see in a moment, subjugation). It is difficult to hold that subjectivation is a way out of subjection, a radical alternative to it. The subjection paradigm, just like that of sovereignty, becomes all-encompassing. Indeed, in the same way in which one does not exit sovereignty by becoming sovereign, one does not exit subjection by becoming a subject, by acquiring a new subjectivity. The alternative to the subject paradigm is the singular, or singularity, where it is understood that the singular is always already plural, and it endures as such in a metastable state of constant vacillation, a state of contingency and rupture. We have seen that individuation as a completed process is impossible and the individual does not exist. The same holds true for the subject and subjectivity. What we have is instead a constant process of subjection, which, just like individuation, never completes itself, and a plurality of exits, or *lines of flight*, as Félix Guattari (2016) and Gilles Deleuze and Guattari (1987) have it, at the recurrent threshold, where the gathering happens and singularization becomes possible. What gathers at the threshold, and possibly defies subjection, is not a series of subjects or individuals, but rather fragments, relations, and dividuals making up the singular, that is, assemblages, or networks. But the singular is always more than the mere composition in the assemblage or network. As in Heraclitus, "The soul has a self-increasing *logos*" (Curd 2011: 45). *Logos*, as Heidegger often says, is the gathering, precisely. Thus, the singular, 'the soul,' is in a constant state of individuation and amplification.

The gathering relations of dividuals become evident today in digital and machinic reality. Maurizio Lazzarato says, "The machinic functions without the 'subject'" (2012: 147). Following Aldo J. Haesler, Lazzarato gives the example of our typical interaction with an ATM machine. He quotes Haesler who says, "What you are asked to do is to react appropriately, react quickly and without making errors, otherwise you run the risk of being momentarily excluded from the system" (Haesler 1995: 206; cited in Lazzarato 2012: 147). We will have more on Haesler in the next chapter. Lazzarato continues, "There is no subject who *acts* here, but a 'dividual' that *functions* in an 'enslaved' way to the sociotechnical apparatus of the banking network" (147–148). He also remarks, "The ATM activates the 'dividual' not the individual" (148). Of course, this is not limited to a few functions and activities, such as interacting with an ATM, but it is more widespread. The machinic assemblage, of which Gerald Raunig (2016) also speaks and which I will consider again later, notably in Chapter Seven, underlines the general ontology of the dividual. Obviously, this is an ontology of subjection, unless the trans-dividual, of which the machinic assemblage is an occurrence, brings about a new singularity. This can happen through an exit, *lines of flight*, from the nostalgia for the individual and subject, and from the capture of number. Lazzarato also refers to Gilles Deleuze who, speaking about machinic subjugation, says, "Individuals become '*dividuals*,' and masses becomes samples, data, markets, or '*banks*'" (Deleuze 1995: 180; cited in Lazzarato 2012: 148). That is the same as saying that singularities are captured and flattened by the politics of number, which today means the politics of the algorithm; in other words, people become numbers, as Kierkegaard (1980: 33) indicates.

Lazzarato speaks of debt/money as social subjection and machinic subjugation, namely, of the way in which the contemporary neoliberal regime of capital "has a 'hold' on subjectivity" (2012: 145). Working with Marx and Nietzsche, he says that this is done by the use of "legal and police 'machines' (Marx)" as well as mnemotechnical 'machines' . . . which work on and manufacture the subject (Nietzsche)" (146). With an important reference to Deleuze and Guattari, he highlights the system's "twofold 'hold' on subjectivity" (149). It is not simply the fact that subjectivity is produced by the system as subjected, but it also produces itself. The twofold 'hold' that debt/money has on subjectivity brings about the two complementary modalities of "social subjection" and "machinic subjugation." The following passage is very important: "'Social subjection' operates molar control on the subject through mobilization of his conscience, memory, and representations, whereas 'machinic subjugation' has a molecular, infrapersonal, and pre-individual hold on subjectivity" (146). Subjection, then, for Lazzarato, addresses only one aspect of the problem, namely the fact that the produced, manufactured subject or individual finds itself in a state of subjection. Although this subject or individual is fictional, that does not mean that it is false or unreal. It does not truly exist, and yet it is made, forced, to exist. Subjection means nothing but the fact that the open process of individuation is brought to a halt, forced into finitude and closure. We have seen in the preceding chapter how individuation, as a completed process, is impossible from the ontological or ontogenetic point of view. It is only through violent means that a finished state of individuation is produced as subjection. The self is made, truly forced into a fictitious type of existence – fictitious because there is no longer any standing out, any infinitizing exit or line of flight, but rather the self is forced to insist upon itself and remain the same. However, Lazzarato goes deeper, if you will, and also addresses machinic subjugation as that which "dismantles the self, the subject, and the individual" (150). It is here that we find the domain of the dividual, which is perhaps an even more palatable target for the society of surveillance and control, the biopolitical scheme of work, debt, and death. Lazzarato says, "The norm, the rule, and the law have a hold on the subject, but none on the dividual" (*ibid.*). This does not mean that the dividual is freer, more liberated than the subject. More simply, the dividual is attached to the machine, part of a network or assemblage. However, it is in this attachment, which is also a being-with and a between, a threshold, that the dividual can finally communicate with the singular, find the meaning and time/space of the singular: a possible ontological shift. Lazzarato is correct in saying that a critique of neoliberalism cannot limit itself to the question of social subjection, but it must address the equally timely question of machinic subjugation. It is here that the new figure of the trans-dividual, not a new subjectivity, but a singularization, becomes possible. What then appears is the translucency of singularization: infinitizing horizons, lines of flight, or shadows of death.

The destructive critique of the subject is not at all a novelty in philosophy today. Indeed, it was one of the main features of Nietzsche's *philosophizing with a hammer*, his destruction of metaphysics, religion, and morality; a destruction of all temples and idols. In a very important passage from Essay One of *On the Genealogy of Morals*, taking issue with the metaphysical distance injected in the phenomenon of creativity and expression by the logic of *ressentiment*, Nietzsche denies the existence of any underlying level of reality, any substratum. He says, "But there is no such substratum; there is no 'being' behind doing, effecting, becoming; 'the doer' is merely a fiction added to the deed – the deed is everything" (Nietzsche 1967: 45). Yet, the doer, the subject, this "subject of fiction," as Arnold Gehlen (1980: 87) says with a reference to the work of Herman Finer, regularly appears as the "immaterial precipitate" (145) of society. To be sure, dealing with the issue of automatisms, Gehlen comes close to the idea of the network, or assemblage of dividuals, the trans-dividual. This is indeed what the "immaterial precipitate of society's present and past experience" (*ibid.*) is. The words 'immaterial' and 'precipitate' make us think, respectively, of Lazzarato and Simondon; the latter especially in relation to transindividual individuation, or, as I prefer, trans-dividuation. What is certain is that the individual, or subject, is nothing but a reflection of various networks of activities and deeds. Like in the ATM illustration mentioned above, decision is suspended or eliminated. Certainly, what is at stake is the meaning of singularity, for habituation and automatism also bring about the danger of disindividuation and alienation. As Gehlen says, within the system of automatism – and certainly even more so with digitalization today – "there is little place for what is distinctive about a given person" (147). Indeed, the distinctive or characteristic traits of any person, their singularity, appear as "unwanted." Gehlen says, "There is little doubt that today's highly rationalized and thoroughly bureaucratized society expects the person to develop, to a large extent, into a 'functionary.' Personal characteristic which hinder such a development appear unwanted, no matter whether possessed by a genius or by a socially maladapted individual" (*ibid.*). The functionary, or the specialist, is the new wanted individual, the new subject, which is a function of servitude to the system, a number within that system. What is *unwanted* is non-disindividuated singularity, that is, whatever is distinctive, yet grounded (or submerged and subverted) in the common, reproducing itself through difference in the common and *as* the common. This is, in sum, as Stefano Harney and Fred Moten call it, the *undercommons*. Indeed, in relation to the system, to be *unwanted* means "to be in but not of" (Harney and Moten 2013: 26). In a sense, this is like turning the logic of inclusion and exclusion on its head, or rather, against itself. Instead of the functionary we may have, from the viewpoint of the system, the dysfunctional personality; instead of the specialist we have the dreamer; yet, both lacking in subjectivity (or subjection), both lacking the capture of the soul, without however being disindividuated, become rebellious bodies, networks of rebellion, relations of neither-objective-nor-subjective, nonsystemic, dysrelations. They are, in a word, singularities. Yet, the singular, "the capacity of expressing oneself" for Gehlen (166), is today "what is most improbable" (*ibid.*). I will return to Gehlen in the final chapter of this book dealing with the question of singularity as personality.

In the age of digital technology especially, the subject paradigm includes both the moments of social subjection and machinic subjugation, as Lazzarato indicates. Dismantling the subject, or the self, replacing the individual, requires a twofold operation, at the molar and the molecular levels. If the manufactured subject, Nietzsche's 'the doer,' can be almost simply dismissed as a mere fiction, the preindividual hold on subjectivity, which is essentially affective in nature, working at the level of the emotions (fear, for instance), is perhaps more difficult to deactivate. These issues have of course already been explored by Michel Foucault with his notion of discipline as "a political economy of detail" (1977: 139). For Foucault, in the eighteenth and nineteenth centuries, disciplines became "methods which made possible the meticulous control of the operations of the body, which assured the constant subjection of its forces and imposed upon them a relation of utility-docility" (137). It is easy to see here how subjection must also employ forms of subjugation. In reality, the "subtle coercion" exercised over the active body, this "infinitesimal power" (*ibid.*), which works on the plurality of instances constituting the body and is "more regular, more effective, more constant and more detailed in its effects" (80), becomes a new *strategy* of power (biopower), superseding the classical model of sovereignty, becoming "a new microphysics' of power" (139), in a word, biopolitics. Foucault understood this dynamics in relation to the power to punish, just as Nietzsche had done; yet, this is a *generalized* form of punishment, a form of pre-punishment, namely, punishing individuals for what they could do, not necessarily for what they might have done. It becomes precisely a form of discipline and control. But discipline and control will be more effective if exercised at the preindividual level. In the digital age, biopolitical power (which does not completely eliminate sovereignty, but sees it in a new light) is intensified and perfected. I will return to this in the next chapter.

To better understand the problem with the notions of subject and subjectivity, as well as the fact that subjection and subjugation are in a way always present in the subject paradigm, we may turn to the work of Martin Heidegger, in particular his "Letter on Humanism," written in 1946 as a critical response to Jean-Paul Sartre's *Existentialism Is a Humanism*. In "Letter on Humanism," Heidegger repeatedly decries "the dominance of subjectivity that presents itself as the public realm" (1977a: 198), "the modern metaphysics of subjectivity" (199), under which language is forced to stand, and any "subjectivizing" (228), which is in essence a reiteration, even "with its Nietzschean and Marxian [and Sartrean] inversions" (215; brackets added), of the main framework of traditional metaphysics, of absolute metaphysics, which, however, is not false, but "belongs to the history of the truth of Being" (*ibid.*). The critique of subjectivity here is the same as the critique of metaphysics and of the traditional doctrine of humanism, whether in its Roman, Christian, Marxian, or Sartrean variety. Heidegger says that "man has strayed into subjectivity" (231), and he supports a different ("other") type of thinking, which is perhaps *less* than philosophy, or metaphysics (taken here to be coterminous with philosophy), but one "that abandons subjectivity" (207). Today, the concept of subjectivity is rather popular, especially in the context of the important notion of the production of subjectivity. It seems that with an adequate grasp of the function of the double genitive in the phrase 'production *of* subjectivity,' the danger of the subject paradigm (subjection/subjugation) can be avoided. Accordingly, it would be possible to simply distinguish between subjection (an obvious phenomenon of capture) and subjectivation (an exit from it), and assign a totally positive value to the latter. Yet, what I argue in this book, and what a reading of Heidegger's "Letter on Humanism" seems to support, is that this is not a satisfactory move if the aim is to bring about the conditions for a shift to a radically different plane, and build *another* world. The "other thinking that abandons subjectivity" (207) is the singular and poetic, in the sense of Hölderlin (as Heidegger often suggests, in "Letter on Humanism" and elsewhere) as well as in the sense of Vico. In this sense, singularity is not at all synonymous with subjectivity, but neither is it a mere replacement of it. To remain with Heidegger, singularity is a "between" (229), a threshold, as I have often pointed out in the previous chapters, and a neither/nor. Yet, differently from Heidegger, I do not think that this "between" relates subject and object, being itself neither one nor the other. Rather, as plural singularity, the "between" itself is the gathering of dividuals at the threshold and the formation of trans-dividual networks or assemblages. It is not even the result, but the very unfolding, or happening, of the ontology of agitation and combination.

Heidegger speaks of "the dominance of subjectivity that presents itself as the public realm" (198) with a reference to his treatment of the "they" in *Being and Time*. I have already spoken about Bernard Stiegler's problematization of the "they" as disindividuation in Chapter 2 above. For Heidegger, the public realm of the "they," and the idle talk that comes with it, should not be seen in a disparaging way. It is rather a type of relation to Being and the world. To say that this relation is *inauthentic* does not, once again, for Heidegger, imply any negative value judgment. As Heidegger says in *Being and Time*, inauthenticity "constitutes precisely a distinctive kind of being-in-the-world which is completely taken in by the world and the *Mitda-sein* [co-existence] of the others in the they" (1996b: 164; brackets added). Yet, the "devastation of language" (1977a: 198), which, as Heidegger says, is "the house of Being" (213), seems to be a direct consequence of the disindividuation taking place in the public, impersonal realm of the "they." Moreover, as Heidegger stresses, this does not simply have an effect on the daily use of language, but "it arises from a threat to the essence of humanity" (198). This brings back the possibility of "a curious kind of 'humanism'" (224–225), one that is not grounded in any *essence* (*essentia*) or, as Sartre would have it, *existence* (*existentia*). In traditional (Platonic) metaphysics, essence precedes existence. Sartre reverses the statement, and he says that existence precedes essence. However, Heidegger warns, "the reversal of a metaphysical statement remains a metaphysical statement" (208). The *other thinking* proposed by Heidegger favors the primacy of neither existence nor essence. Essence, if we can still speak of it (but Heidegger does), is now ek-sistence, namely the ecstatic standing out in the Open, facing the abyss, vacillating at the threshold, with a sense of trepidation. There is trepidation because of the indecision and indeterminacy of ek-sistence, of facing the Open, but also because of the distance from the structure of *care* brought about by the devastation of language, the disindividuation, and the dominance of subjectivity. Introducing the concept of care, to which he devotes much more space in *Being and Time*, Heidegger says, rather poetically, "But if man is to find his way once again into the nearness of Being he must first learn to exist in the nameless" (199). *Care* as such always indicates the possibility of a return – a return to the 'essence,' or more simply *home*. But the return remains improbable and imprecise. Yet, if there is any humanism possible, any *humanitas*, Heidegger says, it must be "meditating and caring, that man be human and not inhuman, 'inhuman,' that is, outside his essence" (200); that is, again, without a home. I will go back to the question of care in Chapter Eight, below.

Just like Louis Althusser's theoretical anti-humanism, Heidegger's thought opposes humanism. But as he says, and this is also true in Althusser's case, "this opposition does not mean that such thinking aligns itself against the humane and advocates the inhuman, that it promotes the inhumane and deprecates the dignity of man" (210). Rather, he continues, "Humanism is opposed because it does not set the *humanitas* of man high enough" (*ibid.*). The problem seems to be that every humanism remains within the framework of metaphysics and subjectivity (202). The human becomes the subject *par excellence*, the decider, and the tyrant of being (210). However, this is not at all what the original place and vocation, the original task and work (*ergon*, to use a wonderful expression by Aristotle) should be, or necessarily is. Heidegger says, "Man is not the lord of beings" (221), and at least twice does he repeat in "Letter on Humanism" his famous assertion, "Man is the shepherd of Being" (210 and 221). It is in this sense that the question of *care* becomes central. With a reference to *Being and Time*, Heidegger says that this is why *ecstatic existence* (or *ek-sistence*), namely, the original human disposition, or even human essence (for ek-sistence is here not opposed to essence), is "experienced as 'care'" (210). Yet, in the age of disindividuation, alienation, disaffection, and homelessness, the distance from the structure of care becomes increasingly important. The manufactured subject or individual of modernity, which is the result of technics of subjection and subjugation, capture and servitude, experiences this distance as a paradoxical condition of carefree attitude. Notions such as creativity and flexibility in life and work give the impression that there are no limits, that nothing is impossible (not in the sense of Parmenides, but in the sense that everything is possible – a sense recently made popular in advertising by the sports brand Adidas).

Yet, the time comes when one of Kierkegaard's conditions of despair, infinitude's despair, namely, lacking finitude, becomes apparent. To lack finitude means to lack a ground, grounding, a foundation, or situation. This is no longer a condition whereby one experiences the Open as concrete projectuality. What one experiences is the merely abstract and fantastic, as well as the abyss – a bad infinitizing process from which there is no return to the finite, and thus no synthesis of finitude and infinitude and no becoming concrete. What happens here is that one is "volatilized in the infinite" (Kierkegaard 1980: 33). For Kierkegaard this is the loss of the self, the "greatest hazard of all" (32), which, however, "can occur very quietly in the world, as if it were nothing at all" (32–33). Alternatively, what can take place is the opposite condition of despair, finitude's despair, namely, lacking infinitude. Instead of complete infinitization, there is here complete finitization. This happens "by becoming a number instead of a self, just one more man, just one more repetition of this everlasting *Einerlei* [one and the same]" (33). To be sure, Kierkegaard's idea of the self is not the one of the tradition of modernity, which develops from Locke and Descartes. First of all, the self is for Kierkegaard always in the making, always individuating and never fully individuated. Moreover, the self is divided; it is a relation and a synthesis – of two (finitude/infinitude, necessity/possibility, and so on), but perhaps, we may add, even more than two. It is then an assemblage of dividuals. Usually Kierkegaard's philosophy is understood as a philosophy of subjectivity. However, here, too, in Kierkegaard there is a fundamental difference from the tradition of subjectivity, the one attacked by Heidegger for instance; it is rather a philosophy of singularity (the same can be said of Sartre's philosophy, pace Heidegger). The self itself, in Kierkegaard, *is* the singular. This becomes absolutely clear in his masterful portrayal of Abraham's paradoxical and tragic experience in *Fear and Trembling* (1985). Abraham chooses to obey God and is ready to sacrifice Isaac, operating a teleological suspension of the ethical. In so doing, he "has, from the single individual, become higher than the universal" (78). Leaving aside the problems likely to be associated with the word 'universal,' the singular universal, which becomes a strong concept in Sartre as well, belongs in a philosophy of singularity. In fact, its phenomenology describes a trajectory of open totalization. This is the same as saying that the singular universal belongs in the logic of becoming and individuation as a metastable process. The singularity of the self is never an accomplished fact, and as such the self itself does never really exist (as a mere being there), namely, it never really *is*; rather its existence has the ecstatic character required by Heidegger, a constant standing out, an exit and a return, not to the same, but to the other, itself as another (as Arthur Rimbaud says),[1] or simply other. Since this never stops (re)occurring, the plurality constituting the singular, constituting the 'self' becomes apparent. For Kierkegaard, "every moment that a self exists, it is in a process of becoming" (1980: 30). He also says, "To become oneself is to become concrete" (*ibid.*). However, this is a process that always remains open. Indeed, "the progress of the becoming must be an infinite moving away from itself in the infinitizing of the self, and an infinite coming back to itself in the finitizing process" (*ibid.*). Here, too, we find metastability and vacillation, and the self as such, as a closed totalization, never obtains.

Descartes himself was on the right track when in an astonishing passage of his Second Meditation, after having established *that* the 'I' is, he asks the question of its *whatness*. This is a very central moment in *Meditations on First Philosophy* because here Descartes problematizes the relationship between existence (that something is) and essence (what it is). The passage in question is, "And so from this point on, I must be careful lest I unwittingly mistake something else for myself" (Descartes 1993: 18). Obviously, for Descartes what I could mistake for myself is not this desk or this smartphone (though technically that could also be a possibility), but rather my own body. Perhaps out of fear for the reality of dividuality, Descartes takes refuge in subjectivity and in the simplicity and unity of the *Cogito,* the 'I think.' That is indeed what I am, "a thinking thing" (19), a "thing that thinks" (20). And so Descartes establishes the subject and subjectivity in modern philosophy. Obviously, this thinking thing (*res cogitans*), just like any other 'thing,' must be made of something. Yet, in this case the 'material' constituting the thing is wholly immaterial; it *is* thought (understood from an idealist viewpoint). So it is not the case that the thing that I am also has the capacity for thinking, the feature of thought. It is not as it is the case, for instance, with Artificial Intelligence where you have a device that has some capacity and autonomy for thinking. I am not a thing to which thought is attached. Rather, this 'I' that I am *is* itself thinking, wholly and inherently (as well as reflectively) constituted by thought: I think that I think. The gathering of dividualities, that poetic con-fusion of bodies, notably present in the thought of Vico and Nietzsche among others, is thus avoided, and the dominance of subjectivity in modernity, a figure of decisionism and sovereignty, begins.

Descartes' argument can be seen as a subjective version of Parmenides' objective argument for the establishing of being. The Milesian thinkers that came before Parmenides, namely, Thales, Anaximander, and Anaximenes, asked the question, 'What is it?' That was the question of the nature of everything, the universe, the cosmos. Answering that question at face value is complicated, or made impossible, by the fact that everything changes. Thus, they formulated a hypothesis: What if behind, underneath, or beyond everything that changes there is something that remains the same? This is the question of the *arkhē*, the principle and common substance of everything. They gave different answers: for Thales it was water, for Anaximander *apeiron* (the boundless), and for Anaximenes air. Then Heraclitus understood that change, or becoming, which seemed to be a problem, was actually the answer to the question about the nature of reality. No need to look further: change, or becoming (or fire), is reality itself. Everything changes, everything flows, yet change itself does not change, but persists and remains: "Changing it rests" (Curd 2011: 46). This is Heraclitus' greatest contribution: to understand that the question itself was actually the answer – a metastable answer. Yet, Parmenides saw that before asking the question of the whatness of things, we should make sure that things are, because they could apparently also not be. So before asking the question, 'What is it?' we should make sure *that* it is. The most fundamental question is then, 'Is it, or is it not?' The answer is unequivocal, and it founds the logic of identity: Yes, it is, and it could not not be. Being is, and it must be; its opposite, nothing, is not, and it cannot be. Indeed, if nothing were, it would be something. There is then no exit from being, from something – *whatever* that is. Yet, after having established *that* it is, the question of its whatness comes up. What is it? This time, it will be neither water, nor air or fire, or any of the other elements; in other words, it will not be anything other than itself – because this would be a contradiction. Rather, it is it itself, "full of what-is," never changing, remaining the same (60).

Just as being is full of what-is in Parmenides, the 'I think' is full of thought in Descartes. Furthermore, we see that, *mutatis mutandis*, the formal argument is the same in both. We first make sure *that* something is; then we ask *what* it is. With Parmenides, the result is the (objective) metaphysics of being (which has been alternatively interpreted in an idealist or materialist fashion). Indeed, for Parmenides there is identity, or at least parallelism (like later in Spinoza), between what is and what can be thought, "for the same thing is for thinking and for being" (58), or "What is for thinking is the same as that on account of which there is thought" (60). With Descartes, the result is the metaphysics of the subject and subjectivity. In a sense, they both deal negatively with the unavoidable problem of change and becoming, which Heraclitus, as well as all dialectical and transductive thinking from Hegel and Marx to Simondon, turns into a powerful tool, an ontological machine of disruption and new composition, of suspension and return (or fall) into the other. Parmenides ends up with a sphere full of being, *and nothing more* – though, it must be stressed, Parmenides' sphere of being, his reality, is paradoxically inclusive of the potential.[2] Descartes arrives at the 'I think' thinking itself: I think that I think; a thought full of thought, master of its own clarity and distinction, its own separation (i.e., its own decision and sovereignty).

Once the metaphysics of the subject, the self, is established in philosophy, it is easily adopted by other fields of knowledge. The distinction between the self, and the other, the non-self, becomes paradigmatic. In an interesting book, *The Limits of the Self* (2012), written at the interface of the philosophy of biology and the philosophy of immunology, Thomas Pradeu shows how this has been precisely the case in biology and immunology, and how problematic this is. The main question of the book is, "What makes the identity of a living thing?" (1) The question is really twofold: it asks about the uniqueness of a living thing and its individuality. The word 'uniqueness' can be understood here as singularity, namely, what "makes a living thing different from all other living things, including those that belong to the same species" (2). The word 'individuality' is related by Pradeu himself to "the problem of individuation" (*ibid*.), which is "a problem of separation, or delineation of the real" (*ibid*.). However, he soon admits the plural (and thus, we might say, dividual) constitution of what then appears to be an individual: "At least in the domain of the living, an individual is never strictly indivisible – contrary to the etymology of the term 'individual'" (*ibid.*). He thus explicitly describes the ontology of the living being as *the unity of a plurality*. He says that "to understand what creates the unity of a living being consists of determining how it is *the unity of a plurality*, which is to say, although it is formed of diverse partially isolatable constituents [i.e., dividuals], the organism is still a unified whole" (*ibid.*; emphasis and brackets added). However, precisely because of its constitution, this unified whole must be understood as a trans-dividual reality, an assemblage or network of different parts. This obviously calls into question the traditional conception of the self in biology, provided by the traditional and dominant self-nonself theory. After critiquing the self-nonself theory, Pradeu proposes the *continuity theory*, capable precisely of taking into account the plural constitution of what then appears as a unity. I think this can also be understood as trans-dividual ontology, present in biological individuation, but also in individuation in general, for instance, in Simondon's psychic and collective individuation.

Pradeu gives the example of a coral reef, asking the question of "what counts as 'one' individual" in it (*ibid.*). He says, "Is a coral one single vast individual whose polyps (each little 'tube' topped with a mouth and tentacles) are so many 'parts,' or should each polyp be considered an 'individual'?" (*ibid.*). This is evidently very similar to Gilles Deleuze and Félix Guattari's concept of rhizome, of which I will say more in a later chapter. For now, it might be important to stress that, it is perhaps not a matter of individual(s) at all. The concept of the trans-dividual should be enough to account for the reality of the coral reef or any other (perhaps living as well as nonliving) assemblage, or singularity. But to say that the plurality of the singular is made of 'parts' or dividuals, in no way diminishes their ontological status; it is rather a recognition of the fact of their necessary (inter)dependence and relationality, which is in itself a prime ontological structure. When I say 'necessary,' I do not mean to imply the exclusion of contingency. In fact, what is *attached* is attached contingently, just like the formation of any event, which could also not happen – and indeed, as Duns Scotus says, it is *caused contingently* (1987: 53–54). Duns Scotus also says, "Contingency arises from motion, which, though it is caused necessarily in so far as it is uniform, gives rise to *difformity* [*difformitas*] owing to its parts" (54; emphasis and brackets added). This *difformity*, which is obviously not 'deformity' but the lack of uniformity, is precisely what belongs in the concept of trans-dividuality, the network or assemblage, and the singular as such. Yet, all this does not make it impossible to think the common. Indeed, Duns Scotus says that "the singularity of a thing is no impediment to the abstraction of a common concept" (32–33). As we have seen in the preceding chapter, singularity becomes actual on the basis of, and because of, the open potentiality of the common. Its abstraction, as Marx shows in the *Grundrisse*, is the method of a return to the concrete.

Pradeu addresses the question of the distinction between uniqueness (or singularity, for us) and individuality, which is what can be numbered. He agrees with Leibniz, for whom two entities are never completely identical – and indeed for Leibniz identity *is* difference. However, he says that *"in practice*, there are entities that *we wish* to *qualify as* 'identical,' particularly in biology" (3; emphasis added). And he gives the example of each clone of a clonal plant. The words I have highlighted in Pradeu's statement above point to the fact that we regularly speak of identity as identification and classification. This may be practically useful, as Pradeu says, especially in a science like biology. However, when this is done, as is regularly done, in the domain of social, political, cultural, and daily life, the results are often devastating; in fact, the reduction of any multiplicity to the one and its consequent capture in categories of (social) identity cannot happen without violence. This is the violence defining the law, the police mentality, the bureaucracy, and so on; it is biopolitics, or the politics of number. In truth, "the ontological question" asked by Pradeu, as to the identity of a living or nonliving being, can only be answered, with Leibniz, by saying that a being's identity is that being's difference, and this difference is itself "a complete world" (Leibniz 1989: 9), a mirror of the whole universe, "multiplied as many times as there are substances [i.e., beings]" (*ibid.*; brackets added).

Pradeu problematizes and ultimately discards the notions of self and nonself which have defined immunology since the 1950s. Immunology itself is "traditionally defined as the science that studies an organism's defense against any foreign entity capable of invading it" (Pradeu 2012: 4). The language of politics and war is here immediately evident. The nonself is the enemy that must be eliminated or destroyed. The self-nonself theory was formulated by Macfarlane Burnet, an Australian virologist, in the 1950s on the basis of a former study he co-authored with Frank Fenner in 1949, in which the notions of self and nonself were introduced in immunology and biology (Pradeu 2012). Pradeu's aim in *The Limits of the Self* is that of determining whether these two notions "effectively constitute a proper foundation for a definition of biological identity" (4). For a series of reasons that I cannot review here, he answers negatively and, as I have mentioned above, proposes the continuity theory as an alternative to the self-nonself theory. The continuity theory is actually based on discontinuity and rupture. Essentially, the theory says that "the triggering of an immune response is due to any strong discontinuity in the expression of antigenic patterns that the organism interacts with" (137). The key, technical, word in Pradeu's continuity theory is 'antigen,' which he defines as follows: "Today, the term *antigen* refers to any molecule (ligand) capable of setting off an immune reaction in an organism" (19–20). It is then "a matter of a rupture in the continuity of molecular determinants interacting with immune cells" (137). An organism's identity is no longer seen as the self's defense from the nonself, but as a metastable process of discontinuity and rupture whereby an organism reacts "to its own components" (135), a "molecular difference" (137). This is surprisingly close to Simondon's theory of transindividual individuation, and this is the reason why it is important for us here. Immunology, as "the discipline that studies *defense*" (16) according to the self-nonself theory, the them/us situation of war, shows itself in fact to be the discipline of the dynamic and constant process of autoimmunity, namely, the fact that "the immune system reacts continuously to endogenous antigens" (85). The rupture in the continuity of molecular patterns means "the appearance of a strongly different molecular pattern" (137). In fact, it is not the foreign nature of antigenic patterns, but their difference and unusual occurrence that triggers an immune response (138–140). Thus, change is not caused by a foreign invasion, as the self-nonself language of the (Schmittian-like) theory of politics and war would have it, but by an inner turbulence, a constant individuating potency that demolishes any illusion of sameness and identity: the self is the other and the other is the self; or rather, there is no self or other, but a plurally constituted singularity, ever-changing and self-multiplying.

Thus, instead of the self-nonself opposition, Pradeu sees immune mechanisms at work everywhere in the living world (25). For one thing, he finds it "astonishing . . . that a discipline as deeply experimental as immunology uses as its central concepts terms which come from psychology and, before that, philosophy – or metaphysics, to be more precise" (42). He also points out how "[a]ccording to the *Oxford English Dictionary*, the first occurrence of 'self' is found in John Locke's *Essay Concerning Human Understanding*" (43). He elaborates on the problematic nature of the self not only in immunology and biology, but in philosophy and in general as well. He reviews important questions such as the question of the relation of a self to an organism or to the 'I,' notably the nature of the relation as having or being a self, and so on (*ibid.*). The problem is indeed general, and one of ontology. The positing of the centrality of the self, the subject, at the beginning of modern philosophy, with Locke and Descartes among others, also produces the critical and deconstructive line of thinking we have briefly seen dealing with Kierkegaard and Heidegger above. But it is a trajectory that goes from Spinoza through Nietzsche to our contemporary awareness of the untenability of a simple, unified, and closed concept, an essence that has the structure of permanence and sovereignty (Spinoza's kingdom within a kingdom, or Nietzsche's sovereign individual), a stable and fixed identity. Thus, reading Pradeu's challenge to the self-nonself theory in immunology and his replacement of it with the continuity theory is very instructive in many ways. The central point of the continuity theory is that *molecular difference* triggers an immune response (139). Thus, molecular difference appears as the main concept as well as the main motor of change. Pradeu says that the terms 'continuity' and 'discontinuity' could also be replaced in the future by other terms. What he rather stresses is the need to discard the notions of self and nonself, the self-nonself theory as a whole, the language of defense and war from the fields of immunology and biology. But the implications of this operation for other domains are apparent. For instance, in political ontology too (and in political thinking in general) the false dialectic of self and other, us and them, friend and enemy, needs to be constantly challenged until it can be discarded. Here, too, a theory of *rupture* and *difference* is more likely to provide us with a more adequate understanding of reality as well as an adequate plan for the future. Otherwise we remain caught within the prejudicial thinking typical of the (state) security paradigm according to which it is necessary to identify (and stigmatize) the nonself, the foreign, the other, keep it at a distance, expunge, or destroy it. In order to do that, and reactively and slavishly (in Nietzsche's sense) find our own pale and sad identity, we accept the building of walls, the proliferation of borders everywhere, the promulgation and application of cruel and inhumane laws, the multiplication of detention centers and prisons and concentration camps, and the triumph of the police mentality everywhere. The result is a situation of subjection and subjugation, the loss of the open singularity and of difference. There is perhaps an illusion, in being a subject thus manufactured, of keeping one's ipseity, or identity. However, ipseity itself, often poorly understood as individual identity, is in reality, just like haecceity (thisness), another way of naming the singular, and it should accordingly be understood on the basis of the common, as an expression of the common. We will return to this in the final chapter of this book. We will see that ipseity is, in fact, a transductive phenomenon/process of contingency, discontinuity, and rupture – not at all a fixed and asphyxiating cage for the conservation of a nonexistent self.

NOTES

1. In a letter to Georges Izambard of May, 13, 1871, Rimbaud says, "I is an *other*" ["Je est un autre"] (See Rimbaud 2008: 113).

2. This is not the place to elaborate on Parmenides' inclusion of the potential in the sphere of what-is, but it might be useful to say a few words about it. In one of the Parmenidean fragments (fragment 6), the Greek word used for 'being' is πέλειν, whose meaning indicates a constant state of agitation and unrest. Because of this, but also because of other reasons that I cannot review here, it is important to think of being as potency, of what-is as what-can-be. One way of saying this is that reality must include possibility, and this is something that even common sense suggests. A stronger claim that can be made is that reality *is* potentiality. Fundamentally, something is because it can be. For Parmenides, what is *can* and *must* be. There is here the ontological convergence of two different (usually seeing as opposite) modalities of being: possibility (or potentiality or contingency) and necessity.

2

Capture

FOUR
Borders and Vortices (Life and Work)

In the previous chapter, we examined the limits of the subject and the self, the possibility that the whole paradigm of subjectivity (including subjection, subjugation, and subjectivation), just like the paradigm of individuality, is the result of (bio)political constructive practices that hide the turbulence of preindividual and trans-dividual reality, its ontological power, and the fact that the trans-dividual (appearing now as an individual) is left, especially with digital technology, in a dispersed situation of isolation and seriality, the dispersal of disindividuation, far from the gathering threshold where the power to act, the singularity, becomes concrete and actual. Yet, the vortex is there, at the threshold, appearing now as a border, as the cracks within the apparent identity of life and work.

The digital society of control acts more on the preindividual dimension of existence than on the manufactured subject or individual. In this sense, (machinic) subjugation comes before (social) subjection; however, the latter is still part of the general paradigm of domination. In a section of *Sociologie de l'argent et postmodernité* called "Au-delá du panoptisme," Aldo Haesler argues that the model of the Panopticon, with its molar hold on the subject, is now superseded by "a complete cartography of our acts" (1995: 99). To be sure, the meticulous and detailed way in which power acts on the body, on its minimal motions and folds, was already described by Foucault in *Discipline and Punish* and other works, and it was at the basis of his idea of a productive, rather than only repressive, type of power. For Foucault, absolute sovereignty yields to new strategies of domination that entail the implementation of new techniques, new disciplines, and ultimately a different modality of control. However, for Haesler, this tendency has deepened and it has become more specific and subtle. And certainly, after twenty-five years from the publication of

Haesler's book, the effects of this tendency, now an established and full-blown reality, are obvious to anyone. Haesler gives the example of the health card (*carte-santé*), but, as he says, any card would work as an equally good example of how we constantly carry *on us* the modality and instrument of our being policed and controlled (102). He says, "The more cards multiply, the more our lesser facts and gestures are registered, recorded, and centralized" (99). But he specifies that "it is not the Big Eye of the Company and of Power that scrutinize us this way" (*ibid.*). The passage from a molar (panoptic) to a molecular modality of control is the passage "from a world submitted to a *rule* to a world submitted to some *procedures*" (100). This happens because, on the one hand, power's "Big Eye is void, without a will or an orientation; on the other hand, its objective is no longer panoptic control" (99). This means that it is not important for power to constantly see everything, but that it is enough (perhaps even more effective) to have a hold on some details and thus operate at the micro-level of preindividual subjugation. For Haesler, this can also be described as a passage from a reflexive modality, still present within panopticism, which allows the possibility of critical thinking, a critical stance, to one in which our practices, actions, and gestures are ordered and scheduled to unfold in a completely unreflexive, namely, thoughtless, way. This is what 'the society of control' is, a system based on procedure, rather than on rule, on the implementation of very complex technical settings (100). Again, this procedure has a hold on preindividual (affective and neurological) reality, "a 'new micro-physics' of power," as Foucault (1977: 139) says, "exercising upon [the body] a subtle coercion . . . : an infinitesimal power over the active body" (137). In a sense, what Haesler does is elaborate on and update the passage from discipline to control already present in Foucault, though he has an interesting, critical perspective on the panopticon model. However, this is not very different from the claim according to which we live today under a regime of virtual, or digital, panopticism. So, more than an overcoming of the panopticon, we have a mutation of its structure and operation. Certainly, the example of the ATM we saw in the previous chapter is still relevant, and the ATM machine itself is today more sophisticated and complex than it was decades ago. Yet, the development of new digital technologies, the smartphone we always carry in our pocket (or in our hand), with its Apps and social networks, only enhances and strengthens the system of surveillance and control, while at the same time providing the possibility of an exit, a line of flight, from situations of capture, not a subjectivation out of subjection and subjugation, but rather the singularization of common thresholds. Here, the system can still be called into question, still *understood* (in Spinoza's sense), and hopefully subverted in its operations and functions; its effectiveness can be reduced or turned against it, its potentials deactivated or turned into the potentiality-not-to of the common and singular: "I would prefer not to," and thus, whenever I can,

I will not. Perhaps breaking the procedure that holds us in subjugation is more difficult than breaking the rule that holds us in subjection, yet the gathering that is implicit in subjugation, can become gathering forces of rupture, breaking through the most unlikely, yet common and singular thresholds.

In Haesler, the health card is just an example to show the passage from the "panoptic hypothesis" (1995: 100) to the modality of *control*, which is "a procedure of internalized control," including "*self-control* and a permanent scrutiny of the self" (*ibid.*), thus subjugation. Haesler says, "The card then is not a simple interface whose only role would be to establish a communication between a technical dispositif and an operator (*opérateur*), but a true instrument of introspection and observation of the self" (102). Haesler's operator, who exercises self-control, can now better be described as the user, a new emerging economic and existential figure. Neither simply a producer nor a traditional consumer, the user is a figure of disindividuation. Attached as a dividual, today no longer simply to the card, but to the digital machine, the user does not exercise self-control because its self is simply lost; rather control is exercised on the user, no longer superimposed on it (as it would be in mere subjection) but through a series of micro-techniques of servitude and subjugation, from the various digital commands, the Apps, the buttons, and the swipes. I prefer to emphasize the figure of the user because the operator is perhaps too close to the subject and subjectivity. The user, on the other hand, itself being used, has no self. The word 'user' is not employed here in a disparaging way. Its lack of a self is not necessarily a negative thing. The user approaches the threshold of singularity, though it falls short of singularization, entangled as it is in the web of required operations. Yet, its lack of a self might be understood as a step forward – a step toward the liberation from absolute subjection, though there remains the network of subjugating forces. The user will have to *adapt to whatever* (I will say more about Giorgio Agamben's use of "whatever" as singularity below). It will have to be flexible (a key word of the digital economy of platform capitalism), malleable, and 'creative.' The user will have to live and work under the injunction to become an entrepreneur of the self, as Lazzarato says. Yet, it is here that, through disaffection, de-disindividuation becomes possible, not in the sense of finding one's self and establishing a new individuality, but in the sense of crossing over into the trans-dividual and singular, the *whatever*, not as a place of despair and alienation, but as the richness of the common. As Giambattista Vico says, the common is the opposite of the certain, that is, the individuated (1968: 93). De-disindividuation does not individuate once again; rather, it trans-dividuates and singularizes.

Admittedly, this is not an easy passage, nor a foregone conclusion. We are certainly far from adequately thinking something like Nietzsche's *overhuman* (*Übermensch*), the creator of new values (rather than the user), of life as a work of art (rather than the identity of life and work). The card, as Haesler says, or the digital machine, will situate me within the norm, warn me if I deviate from it, especially "in the case of the passing of a threshold" (1995: 102), and it will stop working, "destroy itself if I, decidedly, persist in not following its instructions" (*ibid.*). In this sense, just like with the model of sovereignty (which is not eliminated but becomes widespread) here too, control becomes "fragmented and . . . more diffused" (103). What remains is the illusion of independence. In fact, as Haesler says, there is now perhaps the illusion of an even greater independence. He says, "The individual certainly has the *illusion* of a greater independence, but at a closer look, its daily life is submitted to increasingly important pressures, which the individual justifies as the result of its own free choice" (*ibid.*). For Haesler, control becomes now permanent, though less focused and oppressive (*ibid.*); it becomes dispersed and vague (104), yet also more effective. The data-filled, and data-*educated*, algorithms, as Nick Srniceck describes them (2017: 41), will exercise a "fragmented" (Haesler 1995: 103) yet omnipresent and permanent control. This is a paradigm that goes beyond the panopticon, as Haesler contends, or it is a continuation, a new, digital version of the panopticon, described by some theorists (such as Byung-Chul Han) as 'dataism,' or as 'datacracy' by other theorists. It is a passage to a "biometric and digital sovereignty," as Renato Curcio says in a recent book tellingly titled *The Sovereign Algorithm* (*L'algoritmo sovrano*; 2018: 92). What the sovereign and data-fed algorithm produces is a shadow (and shadowy) identity of the user (*utilizzatore*), who remains unaware of it (63). As Curcio explains, the algorithm will gather enough information on the user's "identity multiplicity, its anxieties and fears" (*ibid.*). The shadow identities generated by the algorithm are "expressed in numbers and codes" (64). The aim is that of measurement, the production of "numeric indexes and quantities" (*ibid.*); in fact, the constitution of a shadowy ontology. The result is the common experience of "shared isolation," as the Congolese-born, Belgium-based musician Baloji, who works at the interface of digital technology and traditional culture (or rather, cultural con-fusion), puts it (Pellerin 2019). In his short movie, *Zombie*, one of the characters puts on a T-shirt that says, with a reference to a Facebook notification, "Has Left the Group," a sign of de-disindividuation, or de-serialization (or de-linearization, to point to a concept by Lordon, to which I will go back). It is a sign of the dividual approaching the threshold of the singular, a hint of the possibility of a passage to something other, perhaps the overhuman, perhaps simply the exit from the logic of indexes and numbers. Yet, the danger remains that the user simply be "a docile instrument of the instrument purchased following the illusion of possibly incrementing with a little money its intelligence and freedom" (Curcio 2018: 29). Curcio is here using the example of Alexa, Amazon's virtual assistant, capable of transforming anyone, with some irony of course, into "an enhanced human hybrid with its artificial intelligence" (*ibid.*). Nothing could be more distant from Zarathustra's overhuman than this. In fact, the overhuman goes back to the earth and the body. The body itself becomes "a great reason," as one of the most powerful passages in *Thus Spoke Zarathustra* says. The body is thus a vortex and a threshold, where border itself, as the limit, is eliminated, or rather, become the "between," the "with," the tension, and the bridge. This is the passage by Nietzsche I am referring to, "The body is a great reason, a plurality with one sense, a war and a peace, a herd and a shepherd. An instrument of your body is also your little reason, my brother, which you call 'spirit' – a little instrument and toy of your great reason" (Nietzsche 1978: 34). This is in the section titled "On the Despisers of the Body," where Nietzsche also says, "There is more reason in your body than in your best wisdom" (34–35). Indeed, in contrast to Descartes' positing of the "I think" as a detached, simple, and unified entity, in Nietzsche it is the body itself that thinks, not by saying "I," but by *doing* "I" (34). But this doing is of a tumultuous nature, the doing of becoming and effecting. It can include the hybrid character of the transhuman, but essentially it is a passage to the overhuman after the death of god *and* the death of man. Today, the death of man also means the end of the user as the one being used by the instrument, by things. After all, as Zhuangzi says, if one uses things without being used by them, without becoming a thing, there is no danger, "Let things be, but don't allow things to treat you as just an object, then you cannot be led into difficulties!" (Chuang Tzu 2006: 168). Perhaps today the user is an abuser as much as it is abused. Indeed, it is the threshold (the border) between use and abuse that becomes a concern, where the vortex does not move toward the trans-dividual assemblage of singularity, but weakens and implodes into the false security of the subject, the individual, and the self.

Above, I mentioned the concept of de-linearization with a reference to the work of Lordon. To be sure, in *Willing Slaves of Capital*, Lordon speaks mostly of co-linearization, and at times of pre-co-linearization. He only uses the verb "to de-linearise" once (2014: 141); never the noun de-linearization. Yet, de-linearization is essential in his presentation of the prospect of liberation from servitude and domination. The word co-linearization itself is found in very interesting phrases such as "the co-linearization machine" (2014: 84–85 and 98), "the work of co-linearization" (100), "the subjects of co-linearization" (101), "neoliberal co-linearization" (103), and so on. De-linearization becomes important when co-linearization is confronted by sedition and the "geometry of (de-)capture" (141), and when the power of acting, hijacked and diverted by the phenomenon of co-linearization, comes back (142). But what is co-linearization? It is the result – unstable and shaky, to be sure – of the "obsession with alignment" (36) characterizing the desire of the boss, or, Lordon stresses, the *director*. It is indeed, "the desire to turn the enlisted powers into a faithful extension of one's own power" (*ibid.*). It is a meta-desire, the master-desire, namely, "the fantasy of making others identical to oneself" (*ibid.*). Co-linearization is the way in which the ontological powers of acting are enlisted and aligned by the desire of the master; in other words, it is the way in which the singularity of these powers is reduced to number. In this sense, as Lordon says, capitalism becomes a *"regime of desire"* (49; original emphasis). Here, we find, once again, the modality of subjugation, alongside subjection. In Lordon's terms, this means that there are here deeper subjective structures of control, "inscriptions inside individual psyches" (*ibid.*). The preindividual turbulence of the affects is "steered toward specific ends" (51), put to work in and by the system of neoliberal production, which includes the production of subjectivity and the self – and of the entrepreneur of the self. The figure of the entrepreneur of the self is similar to the joyful auto-mobiles of which Lordon speaks, namely, "employees who occupy themselves of their own accord in the service of the capitalist organization" (53). This is what co-linearization is capable of accomplishing. Yet, the consent is only apparent. It is in reality the effect of a passionate, rather than voluntary (this is one of Lordon's main points), acceptance of a condition which is ultimately one of servitude, the effect of subjection *and* subjugation. As Lordon importantly says, "the false transparency of consent is a symptom of the metaphysics of subjectivity" (54). We are back to the main point under discussion here: the metaphysics of subjectivity includes the false passage to subjectivation. The production of subjectivity, the entrepreneur of the self, or the auto-mobile agent, remains caught within the paradigm of subjection and subjugation, a paradigm that has to do with "the mystery of power [*pouvoir*] as 'action on actions,' as the art of *making others do something*" (*ibid.*; brackets and italics in the original). In fact, it is only through singularization, the infinitizing moment, the step into the open and common, that assemblages of dividuals and collectives can found something new. The production of fictions such as the self, the subject, and so on – which, though fictional, are not inconsequential and fake – relies on the employment and recognition of moments such as consent. But, Lordon says, from a Spinozist point of view, "consent does not exist" (55). Consent is often a disguised form of coercion or compulsion. It is always the result of forces that determine one to act in a certain way. Singularization is the way in which these forces (which are affective in character) are *understood* and *mastered*, setting off a new direction, a direction *without directors*, a turn toward liberation from all domination and all capture.

An interesting take on the question of the relation between capture (or servitude) and liberation, subjection/subjugation (including subjectivation) and singularization can be found in Richard Gilman-Opalsky's *Precarious Communism* (2014), especially in the section on freedom and mystification and the mystification of freedom. Gilman-Opalsky also uses the concept of mobility, alongside that of autonomy. *Autonomy* is for Gilman-Opalsky the alternative to capital's "purely ideological and brazenly self-serving definition of freedom" (40). It is "a conception of freedom more robustly defined for the autonomy of everyday people, which invokes *our* mobility – not the mobility of capital – *our* ability to stretch ourselves out toward what we desire to be, to do, to become" (*ibid.*). On the one hand, we can relate this to Lordon's notion of joyful auto-mobiles, who lack real autonomy and are part of the mobility of capital, its subjectivized expression, which has nothing to do with true freedom or singularity. Another concept that could be used to describe this false mobility and autonomy is that of alienation in the sense used by Marx in the *Economic and Philosophical Manuscripts* and in that used by Lordon, for whom "alienation is our most ordinary condition, and out most inexorable one" (2014: 58). But it is also a matter of disindividuation, of a total situation of capture within finitude and dividuality. On the other hand, what is truly important in the passage quoted above, in the notion of "*our* mobility," is the possibility of the open, the threshold, not the border, the force of desire, the tension inherent in doing (the power of acting) and becoming. Writing from an autonomist perspective, Gilman-Opalsky stresses the importance of freedom as autonomy, and "the maximum of autonomy is self-governance" (2014: 105). He pointedly asks the question, "*Does freedom exist if one is only free to do those things one does not want to do?*" (*ibid.*; original emphasis). Yet, it is singularity, rather than subjectivity, that is really being pointed out here. In fact, although Gilman-Opalsky does not use the word 'trans-dividual,' the alternative type of freedom presented by him is indeed the result of the clarity of trans-dividuality. In fact, Gilman-Opalsky addresses the very important question of the relationship between individual and collective action. This is so because autonomous action may at first sight seem to be an individual matter. Yet, we know that the individual must be replaced, being largely a fictional entity. A new conception, closer to reality, will be that of the assemblage, the network, or trans-dividual. Gilman-Opalsky does speak of "autonomous actions that are impossible to target by opponents looking for the central nervous system of our rhizomatic efforts" (41), where the Deleuze/Guattari word 'rhizomatic' has a clear conceptual assonance with 'trans-dividual.' Gilman-Opalsky mentions "mass actions like those in Paris in 1968, in Seattle in 1999, in Genoa in 2001, or in Oakland, CA in 2011" (*ibid.*), and many more recent and current mass actions could be added, such as the Gilets Jaunes and presently the Gilets Noirs in Paris – the latter, an expression of the *sans papiers* movement, perhaps one of the best illustrations of Jacques Rancière's notion of *the part of those who have no part* (Rancière 1999). The important question, however, is that obviously there is no choice that must be made between individual and collective action. From a trans-dividual (or transindividual) point of view, it is the threshold of the common and the singular, the tension, the vortex, and the *between* that replaces the false dichotomy of individual and collective. Gilman-Opalsky points that out as he also remarks on the question of organization versus spontaneity in relation to the fundamental concept of singularity. Thus, he says, "these collective actions may be large and even highly coordinated or organized, and at the same time they may be fully beyond the control of political parties and unions, and they may have no cohesive agenda, despite the best efforts of some of the participants to establish one" (*ibid*.). Perhaps this was precisely the case with the Occupy Wall Street movement that began in Zuccotti Park, New York, in September 2011, and of its many ramifications. But it is also true of the very important actions around the question of migration, both in the Mediterranean Sea and at the US-Mexico border. The 'caravans' of migrants moving through Mexico from Central America regularly challenge the policies of the US government, and the NGOs' rescues of migrants in the Mediterranean Sea regularly disobey the 'closed ports' policy of the right-wing government of Italy, infuriating its (now former) interior minister and other reactionary politicians. These two situations around the reality of migration clearly show that borders are really rhizomatic thresholds of passage and that, as such, they belong in the open, the singular and common. Indeed, the difference between a border and a threshold is that at the border one is intimated to stop, while the threshold is by its very nature an invitation to a passage. The passage is then rhizomatic, not clandestine. It is in this sense that we can read Gilman-Opalsky's use of the concept of singularity, as "expressions of disaffection" that underscore the ontological power of de-disindividuation and de-linearization. Gilman-Opalsky says, "Autonomous expressions of disaffection can be unpredictable, spontaneous, and dangerous, which is what makes them both effective and affective" (41–42). And he continues with a definition of singularity that implicitly engages the political ontology of trans-dividuality. He says, "Within this context, the term 'singularity' does not connote the individual person, but rather, singular expressions of disaffection and desire that may or may not link up with other singularities in a unified way" (42). The moment of unpredictability, indeterminacy, and contingency calls into question the politics of number, of the certain (as Vico says) or individuated. Disaffection and desire are felt at the preindividual level, and from there they proceed, in a rhizomatic fashion, to the threshold, where the gathering occurs.

Disaffection and desire have the power of breaking the *joyful obedience* present at the center of Lordon's analysis and description of the neoliberal condition. With a reference to Foucault, Lordon says that power is "an *art of making others do things*" (2014: 61), and this "is precisely the effect of affects" (*ibid*.). It is in this sense that power is "the totality of practices of co-linearization" (*ibid*.). He uses here, and elsewhere, Spinoza's notion of *obsequium*, that is, Lordon says, "the complex of affects that makes subjected bodies move towards the objects of the norm, namely, that makes subjects . . . do the actions that conform to the requisites of the perseverance of the sovereign's rule" (*ibid.*). He also points out that 'subjects' is "understood here in the sense of *subditus*, not *subjectum*, the subject *of* the sovereign rather than the sovereign subject" (*ibid.*). We have already seen how even the subject as *subjectum*, the result of subjectivation, remains caught within the paradigm of subjection and subjugation. Indeed, to call this figure 'sovereign subject,' especially from a Spinozist angle, might be problematic, as this figure is ultimately fictional. Instead, it is disaffection that operates a turn away from the direction of *obsequium* and de-linearization. As Lordon says later in the text, a passage to which I return in Chapter Seven, it is indignation that breaks with *obsequium* and leads to sedition (140). In an interesting use of Spinoza's passions of sadness and joy (brought about, respectively, by a decrease and an increase of power as *potentia*), Lordon indicates that what produces the indignation whereby de-linearization becomes possible, Gilman-Opalsky's disaffection, is the apparently negative affect of sadness. In Chapter One, we saw the power of the negative as nonaction and as Bartleby's "I would prefer not to." Indeed, Bartleby's attitude and utterance is precisely what challenges coercion. Even when there is ultimately an appearance of consent, when something is done against one's will, or better against one's desire or preference, it is not done with joy, but with sadness. Yet, in a dialectical fashion, this decrease of power turns into a potential increase of power, perhaps touching the threshold of its ontological source. For Lordon, "although we are all equally enslaved to our passions and chained to our desires, to be happy with one's chains is evidently not the same as to be saddened by them" (63). It is in the latter case that joyful obedience ceases to be a possibility, and the possibility-not-to, the preference-not-to, becomes a concrete alternative. Lordon says, "'Coercion' and 'consent' are simply the names that the respective affects of sadness and of joy assume inside institutional situations of power and normalization" (*ibid.*). In sadness, one experiences the desire of freedom, which, as Machiavelli says, defines the condition of the multitude, not of the institutionally powerful, of the elite. Certainly, it is not the desire of those that Lordon calls "the enlisters" (the bosses), for the desire of freedom must always include the freedom of the other. In Machiavelli, this becomes clear in the *effective truth* that the multitude (or the people) do not have a desire to dominate, as the elite do, but only a desire "*not to be dominated, and consequently a greater desire to live in the enjoyment of freedom*" (1950: 122; emphasis added). Freedom is then the desire not to be dominated as well as the desire not to dominate others. This also means respecting (or caring for) the freedom of others. This is a situation that goes beyond coercion and consent, an exit from "all the situations of capture" (Lordon 2014: 98).

This exit has the form and power of singularity. It is an exit from the false dichotomy of coercion and consent, but also from the spurious identity of life and work. Insofar as it is an exit, it has the structure of a neither/nor, of *whatever*. Singularity, as Giorgio Agamben says in *The Coming Community* (1993), is neither individual nor universal. In "its being *such as it is*" (1; original emphasis), it relates to *whatever*, which is, for Agamben, the "coming being" (*ibid*.). Obviously, the coming being is what comes to be, becoming. Singularity is not individuation (as a finished process), but *the individuating* (the open process itself). As whatever being, singularity has, Agamben says, "an original relation to desire" (*ibid*.). But "whatever," Agamben explains, does not mean "it does not matter which, indifferently," which is what the common and technically correct translation tells us. Instead, it means "being such that it always matters" (*ibid*.). It is this type of passage that characterizes the disaffected user, who is a trespasser, and the community of users, or trespassers. It is here that de-linearization and trans-dividuality present themselves as a concrete alternative; it is the passage from a world of alienation and capture (through subjection and subjugation), which always requires the presence of a manufactured self, to the indeterminacy of the open, which always matters. As the algorithm of singularity – "the matheme of singularity," says Agamben, using a Lacanian term – *whatever* (*quodlibet*, in Latin), that which always matters, is what makes it possible to conceive "the individuation of singularity" (16). This type of individuation, and the singularity which unfolds with it, does not point toward the essential, but remains "absolutely inessential" (18), in a way that is similar to the notion of the ontology of the accident in Catherine Malabou, to whom we return in Chapter Six, below. It is a *haecceity*, a thisness, which does not constitute any identity, but remains on the terrain of difference as difference. It is an exit, a line of flight, and, to use Simondon's language, a *transductive, structuring operation* of existence. Agamben is here referring to Spinoza's understanding of the common, especially to "the divine attribute of extension," common to all bodies (*ibid*.). He says that, according to Spinoza, "what is common cannot in any case constitute the essence of the single case" (*ibid*.). This is what Spinoza says in *Ethics*, Part II, Proposition 37: "That which is common to all things . . . , does not constitute the essence of any other particular thing." This is also a statement about trans-dividuality, and it denies the validity of the logic and politics of identity. For Agamben, what is "[d]ecisive here is the idea of an *inessential* commonality, a solidarity that in no way concerns an essence" (18–19; original emphasis). This is a great lesson for any anti-essentialist type of thinking. The denial of any essential commonality is also the denial of identity; it is the singularity of the inessential and of difference. As Agamben importantly says, "*the communication of singularities in the attribute of extension, does not unite them in essence, but scatters them in existence*" (19; original emphasis). 'The communication' is the between, the threshold; the 'singularities in the attribute of extension' are bodies; the fact that they are not united in essence, but scattered in existence, is a claim about the trans-dividual nature of relations without subjects, of inessential (or contingent) assemblages, and of existential networks. The trans-dividual itself, Agamben's whatever, is, to paraphrase Agamben, in-different with respect to properties, but this is precisely "what individuates and disseminates singularities" (*ibid.*). For instance, to stay with the notion of whatever as "being such that it always matters" (1), the Black Lives Matter movement does not point to an essence or identity that must be granted recognition as such, but to the existential conditions of the plurality *and* singularity of black (and brown) bodies under a regime of white power and supremacy, that is, an essentialist and identity-based form of sovereign violence that, contrary to what Spinoza says in the quote above, claims that the common constitutes the particular. The same is true of the movement and dissemination of bodies in the so-called crisis of migrants and refugees at the global level, which is truly the crisis of borders and nation-states. Here, too, there is, not the memory of an essence, but the project of an exit, as well as the unwillingness to remain within, a situation of capture and oppression. It is not the case that migrants and refugees undergo a process of subjectivation out of subjection and subjugation, but rather they enter whatever singularity, which by definition defies any border, and in so doing they call into question the essentialist metaphysics of subjectivity on which the sovereignty of the modern nation-state rests. As Agamben says in an important passage of *Homo Sacer*, which I quote in its entirety, "If refugees (whose number has continued to grow in our century, to the point of including a significant part of humanity today) represent such a disquieting element in the order of the modern nation-state, this is above all because by breaking the continuity between man and citizen, *nativity* and *nationality*, they put the originary fiction of modern sovereignty in crisis. Bringing to light the difference between birth and nation, the refugee causes the secret presupposition of the political domain – bare life – to appear for an instant within that domain" (1998: 131). The border becomes a vortex that produces singularities. Bare life, whose inclusion within the concerns of politics starts the biopolitical paradigm, is always included "in the form of the exception, that is, as something that is included solely through an exclusion" (11), a double exclusion and exception. Yet, bare life, which is common to all living bodies, cannot constitute the essence of the singular. The existence of the singular, its standing out and moving away and forward, has nothing to do with the memory or ground of any essence and with the metaphysics of subjectivity. In truth, the relation between man and citizen, nativity and nationality, birth and nation, is now in question. The exception becomes the norm. But it belongs to the concept and destiny of the norm to be disrupted. The strong (and tempting) injunction to become a subject – thus, to be normalized – clashes with the structure of the ban, "which excludes in including" (77), turning subjectivation into a new form of subjection, normalization into marginalization, and newly acquired identity into a stigma. The true exit of singularization has, to use Agamben's metaphor, the indifference to the common and proper typical of the human face, "whatever face" (1993: 19). For Agamben, "in a face, human nature continually passes into existence, and it is precisely this incessant emergence that constitutes its expressivity" (20). This expressivity is, of course, difference as difference, singularity as such. In-difference only belongs in the structure of the neither/nor of the common and proper. But the emergence into existence, the mode of expression, is the singular, which is every time different, as Leibniz also shows. Agamben says that what is engendered in this passage is whatever being, namely, that which always matters. This is what in *Earthly Plenitudes* is called the *dignity of individuation*, that is, the fact that every existent has dignity in being individuated as such, in its proper individuating process, or singularization (Gullì 2010). For Agamben, "the manner in which [whatever being] passes from the common to the proper and from the proper to the common is called usage – or rather, *ethos*" (1993: 20; brackets added). The word "usage" accentuates the importance of the concept of the user we have been referring to here, but it will also come back in our reading of a passage from Heidegger's essay on the Anaximander fragment in Chapter Six, below. The singular and trans-dividual user has, as its *ethos*, the form and manner of an incessant passage, a constant vacillation and indeterminacy that shun possession and accumulation (*la part maudite*), remaining at the border – really, the threshold – of gathering and assembling. In sharp contrast to the entrepreneur of the self, or any other form of subjectivation, the user (a modern Taoist or Franciscan, though digital, figure) experiences poverty and simplicity as *what matters*, as dignity. In this sense, what comes to the fore is not the identity of life and work, but their in-difference to the forms of value (exchange value and surplus value) as well as to productivity and unproductivity, work and nonwork. The vortex at the threshold is then the experience of *whatever life*. It is not subjectivation, but singularization. Singularity is a process, not a subject.

In a short essay called "What Is a Border?" Étienne Balibar shows the inherent complexity of such a concept as well as the problematic task of trying to define it. What seems to be its obvious meaning, for instance, that of a limit, can easily be shown to be incorrect. For Balibar, to begin with, "we need to overturn the false simplicity of some obvious notions" (2002: 76). This simplicity is arrived at through a process of reduction and many instances of suppression. In relation to the border, this has to do, for Balibar, with "the establishment of definite identities, national or otherwise" (*ibid.*). In his next sentence, he significantly speaks of identities as identifications. In the present work, we are also paying a lot of attention to the question of identity and identification and to the institutional violence behind these constructs. Identity appears here as the politics of number, the subject of policing. By contrast, singularity is the negation of mere identity ('mere' in the sense of non-dialectical) and especially of identification. It is the plurality, or multiplicity, of the singular that becomes a matter of identity only insofar as it is "subject to a forced definition" (*ibid.*). The notion and the constructed (yet not false) reality of the border is a powerful instrument, a *method*, as Sandro Mezzadra and Brett Neilson (2013) say, for the construction of identities, and vice versa, the construction of identities aids in the making of borders. (I will go back to Mezzadra and Neilson's work in Chapter Seven, below). The same condition of violence that establishes borders and grants or imposes identities can also deny or suppress them. This is an expression of the logic of inclusion and exclusion, which, as we have seen above, is called into question by instances of (necessary) existential and political insurgencies, such as the so-called migrant or refugee crisis. Balibar says, "In utter disregard of certain borders – or, in some cases, under cover of such borders – indefinable and impossible identities emerge in various places, identities which are, as a consequence, regarded as non-identities" (2002: 77). But perhaps Balibar's most important point is that "borders cease to be purely external realities" (78). Indeed, as he says in another essay, "The Borders of Europe," included in the same volume, "Borders are vacillating" (92). In "What Is a Border?" he also says that "*some borders are no longer situated at the borders at all*" (84; original emphasis). What I am trying to convey here when I speak of borders and vortices is similar to Balibar's point that borders are today "situated everywhere and nowhere" (78). With a reference to Fichte, Balibar speaks of "inner borders" and "*invisible borders*" (*ibid.*; original emphasis). Furthermore, borders "do not have the same meaning for everyone" (81). This is what Balibar calls the *polysemic nature* of borders. But the general task of borders is to police the population, "*differentiate* between individuals in terms of social class" (82; original emphasis), at the national and international levels, and thus discriminate. The dual interest of the state to control and police its own population while at the same time pretending to protect and favor it – something that may loosely correspond to or, in any case, be related with, internal and external sovereignty – leads to, as Balibar says, "the contradictory position of having both to relativize *and* reinforce the notion of identity and national belonging, the equation of citizenship with nationality" (*ibid.*). As we have seen above, the movements of migration and those of singularization (such as Black Lives Matter or the Gilets Noir) challenge all institutional policies and assumptions from the perspective of a philosophy of radical democracy. These movements can rightly be called (necessary) insurgencies. Generally speaking, their aim (with all due differences) is the demise of the regime of the border at all levels of social and political life: the border as a limit and, as Balibar says, as "almost a home" (83), which is when one becomes a border by constantly residing in it. But it is also an attack against the metaphysics of subjectivity and the cruelty of identity engendered by it. Indeed, what matters is not subjectivity or identity, but singularity, which retains within itself the ontology of its plural and common constitution and remains open to the common and plural. In this sense, the border becomes a threshold. At the end of his essay, Balibar warns against the danger of "the pursuit of a 'borderless world' in the juridico-political sense of the term" (85). The reason for this is that "[s]uch a 'world' would run the risk of being a mere arena for the unfettered domination of the private centres of power which monopolize capital, communication and, perhaps also, arms" (*ibid.*). As we will see in Chapter Seven, Mezzadra and Neilson tend to agree with this important point. Indeed, as becomes increasingly clear today, the work of NGOs and human rights organizations – perhaps what Balibar calls "interpreters, mediators" (*ibid.*) and what has been traditionally belittled and derided by the established revolutionary left— turns out to be essential and absolutely revolutionary; to make just an example, think about the activities of rescue of migrants in the Mediterranean Sea by *Mediterranea – Saving Humans* in the last year or so. In the context of the discourse we are developing here, it is clear that this (as well as many other similar ones) is an instance of the assemblage and amplification of the singular, or singularities, the trans-dividual machine directed toward the dismantling and reshaping of the world. What takes place at the border, or at any gathering threshold, is probably not a struggle between subjection and subjectivation, but rather between subjection and the exit from the entire paradigm of subjectivity (which includes and is grounded in the now obvious, now hidden possibility of subjection), as well as the exit from the violent logic of identity, or better, identification. This (attempted or successful) exit is what may be called singularity, or singularization.

FIVE
Politics of Disposability and Cruelty

In *Disposable Futures*, Brad Evans and Henry Giroux (2015) present a scathing picture of the cruelty and violence inherent to neoliberalism – a structural, systemic, and normative violence and a spectacular cruelty. They begin with a critique of violence, whose purpose is to both describe the ugliness of the neoliberal regime and point, from the authors' perspective of critical pedagogy, in the tradition of Paulo Freire, to new directions. To develop a critique of violence is, for Evans and Giroux, the greatest task today. They say, "Only then might we grasp the magnitude and depths of suffering endured on a daily basis by many of the world's citizens" (3). Indeed, the crisis is global, or global and local (glocal, to use a term we have seen in Chapter One, above); it is economic, political, and cultural, investing all aspects of daily life, and it is a creation of the neoliberal regime – though it ultimately becomes that regime's own crisis and, hopefully, demise. In any case, for Evans and Giroux, it is imperative to "move beyond the conceit of a neoliberal project, which has normalized violence ... [and] reignite a radical imagination" (3–4) capable of rethinking "the meaning of global citizenship in the twenty-first century" (4). Indeed, as they point out, systematic violence is not an exceptional feature of the neoliberal stage of capitalism, but it belongs "in the history of capitalistic development" as a whole (4–5). In this sense, they quote "David Harvey's apt description of capitalist expansion as 'accumulation by dispossession'" (4–5). Harvey's notion of *accumulation by dispossession* stresses the ongoing nature of the process of accumulation, and thus the ongoing nature of the violence inherent to it (Harvey 2003). Accumulation is the precondition of capitalist development – a precondition that for Marx is grounded in the history of "conquest, enslavement, robbery, murder, briefly force" (1977: 507), a history "written in the annals of mankind in letters of blood and fire" (508). This is the history of *expropria-*

tion, Marx says, and it is what Harvey's 'accumulation by dispossession' also addresses. But this history, as Harvey's rephrasing of "primitive accumulation" intends to emphasize, must be constantly renewed and its (structural and systemic) precondition posited again and again. After all, this is the meaning of the real subsumption, which today invests all aspects of life. Evans and Giroux say that the neoliberal regime is "precisely organized for the production of violence" (2015: 5). This means that it concerns itself with the renewal of the history of and preconditions for further accumulation and expropriation. But it must do so in a changed landscape that includes digital technology, the financialization of daily life, the identity of work and life (the 24/7 economy, with its increasing mode of precariousness), the biopolitical and thanatopolitical paradigm of surveillance and control, which, in a sovereign manner, decides about everybody's life and death; hence, the disposable futures, of which Evans and Giroux speak. However, they add with a reference to Frantz Fanon, there remain forms of powerful and collective resistance that "violence . . . cannot deal with, except by issuing more violence" (6). And there also remains Walter Benjamin's *real emergency*, to which I will return below.

In a manner similar to Lordon's emphasis on desire, Evans and Giroux indicate that, essentially, the normalization of violence has to do with forms of affective, passionate capture, "a politics of desire and the production of subjectivities in the interest of their own oppression" (21). This is the same as what Lordon calls co-linearization, as we have seen in the previous chapter. Evans and Giroux stress the manipulation of desire that happens through the spectacle (with references to Guy Debord) and "the seductions of violence," as the title of one section of their book reads (20–33). However, here too, we find the twofold dimension of capture and exit, fear and courage, servitude and rebellion. The production of subjected and subjugated individuals is only one aspect of the situation; the other is the threshold of the singular, the exit and line of flight into an alternative way of living and thinking. Of course, there is despair, but there must also be hope. The subjugated individual may even not be aware of its condition of despair at all, as Kierkegaard already showed. Yet, the disaffected individual, who is at the threshold of the singular and thus shedding its fictional and forced individuality, may turn the experience of despair into a creative act of hope. This is evident in the potential use of digital technology, social media, and the logic of the spectacle. As we have seen, this technology also has a twofold dimension: on the one hand, it is a means of surveillance and control; on the other, it can be used in subversive ways. Evans and Giroux say, "Individuals' capacity to create and globally distribute imagery, first-person accounts, and live video streams . . . are continually transforming relationships between politics, spectacular violence, and possibilities for community resistance to oppression, as has been the case in Ferguson, Missouri" (21–22). Another notable instance of this possibility is the 'Eric Garner video' of the summer of 2014 in Staten Island, New York. Ramsey Orta, the courageous young man and Garner's friend who videotaped Garner's fatal encounter with the police, is a perfect example of de-linearization and singularization. Sadly, there are terrible consequences to actions of this type, and Orta is the only person involved in the Eric Garner case to be serving time in prison. He was arrested on charges unrelated to the Garner case; yet, soon after his video was made public, he became the target of regular harassment by the police. Subversive actions, of an individual or collective type, easily become the target of the intensification of institutional violence; yet, they also show its degree of normalization and its spectacular and fascistic structure and operations. Evans and Giroux point out that it is of course not the case that the recent change in media and technology has brought about "a more democratic society" (28). Yet, it "generates new modes of appropriation and production, [and] radicalizes the conditions for creating critical forms of social agency and resistance" (29). What is thereby produced, at the political and social level, is the figure of the disaffected and trans-dividual user, desiring to escape the condition of passionate servitude and capture, facing the danger, rather than capitulating to fear. This is, I quote again, what "violence . . . cannot deal with, except by issuing more violence" (6). It is a dialectical struggle, similar to the one encountered in Hegel's section on the master/slave dialectic. In this sense, it is also a question of new ethical formations, "the creation of counter-cultures," as Evans and Giroux say (41), in which violence is not avoided altogether, but is engaged "with the ethical care and consideration its representation and diagnosis demand" (*ibid.*). They quote Primo Levi, who stresses the importance of one's power to refuse consent (42). But refusing one's consent, even in the form of a suspended potentiality as one finds it in Bartleby's "I would prefer not to," always includes the fact of facing, and thus countering, violence, rather than avoiding it altogether. Indeed, the latter situation would be impossible in a world of systemic and normalized violence. At the outset of *The Wretched of the Earth*, Fanon says that "decolonization is always a violent phenomenon" (2004: 34). The same is true of de-linearization, singularization, or any process of liberation. This does not mean that trans-dividual singularities will engage in acts of violence. Essentially, singularity is love. Yet, what this means is that these new singularities cannot avoid confronting, through civility and care (i.e., through antiviolence, as we will soon see with Balibar), the structure of normalized and, today, spectacular, violence. Insofar as this type of violence is both the substance and the expression of the law, confronting it means engaging in what Walter Benjamin calls the "law-destroying" function of "divine violence," which "is lethal without spilling blood" (Benjamin 1978: 297). In the trajectory of our ontology, but in line with the critical pedagogy approach of Evans and Giroux, this amounts to a remaking of the structure and spirit of the world. It is of course a utopian strain of thinking that leads to this, but it is also the only exit from the dystopian imagination (Evans and Giroux 2015: 12–20) that is preparatory to spectacular violence and the current zombification of politics and culture (17).

In *The Wretched of the Earth*, the aim of decolonization is the construction of a new humanity (35). This remains true today in the age of disposability and the evisceration of the human, as Evans and Giroux note. Disposability, which they prefer to Zygmunt Bauman's concept of 'waste,' is engineered by biopolitical (and thanatopolitical) "machineries of social death" (45) geared toward the production, precisely, of "disposable humans," Zygmunt Bauman's expression, quoted by Evans and Giroux (46), and bare life. Physiological death, as Michel Foucault also argues in *"Society Must Be Defended,"* does not have to be the necessary outcome of biopolitical violence; social death is also common. When the State functions in the biopolitical mode, *racism* becomes the way in which "the old sovereign right to kill" (Foucault 1997: 256) is once again exercised. This is evident today around the question of migration, both in Europe and in the US, where sovereigntist rhetoric and policies regularly show their racist underpinning. According to Foucault, this is so because in the biopolitical mode, "racism alone can justify the murderous function of the State" (*ibid.*). Racism is "the precondition that makes killing acceptable" (*ibid.*). Indeed, racism is the reason and the outcome of "a world divided in two," as Fanon says (2004: 3). It justifies enhanced measures of security, such as the recently approved Security Decree-bis in Italy or the projected wall at the US-Mexico border, as well as greater police surveillance and repression, the suspension of freedoms and rights, the closure of ports, the creation of detention or concentration camps, and so on. As Foucault says, "the murderous function of the State" does not entail "simply murder as such," but "also every form of indirect murder," such as "exposing someone to death, increasing the risk of death for some people, or, quite simply, political death, expulsion, rejection, and so on" (*ibid.*). *Homo sacer*, the life that can be taken at will, the person who can be killed but not sacrificed, as Agamben (1998) shows, is always inscribed within a racist paradigm. Genocidal extermination, which for Agamben takes place in the dimension of biopolitics, is a matter of bare life, the extermination of bare life (Agamben 1998: 114), which is the foundation of biological racism. Fanon's world divided in two is a world in which the colonized and oppressed are reduced (or reducible) to bare life. For Foucault, racism "first develops with colonization, or in other words, with colonizing genocide" (1997: 257). What he then calls *modern racism*, which, he says, is not merely a matter of ideology and hatred, but is "bound up with the technique of power, with the technology of power" (258), the *new racism* of biopower, is a development of the logic of colonization into the neoliberal politics of disposability. The need for the construction of a new humanity remains as urgent in the age of disposability as it was in previous times. The normalization of violence and of war as a "state of exception" (Evans and Giroux 2015: 50), namely, the extension of war into daily life, is the truth of the "machinery of disposability" (48–53), which is essentially a racist dispositif of power, of biopower. This entails "a global colonization of the imagination" (65), the alienation of singularity, and a war not only on the other as other but also on the other within the self. For Foucault, in modern times "war will be seen not only as a way of improving one's own race by eliminating the enemy race . . . , but also as a way of regenerating one's own race" (1997: 257). This means that the interest of the biopolitical State will be twofold: "the elimination of races and the purification of the race" (258). This is the way in which sovereign power is exercised once again.

Walter Benjamin says, "in the exercise of violence over life and death more than in any other legal act, law reaffirms itself" (1978: 286). This violence is, for Benjamin, "both lawmaking and law-preserving violence" (*ibid.*), and it finds special and ignominious expression in the police. Benjamin says that "this ignominy lies in the fact that in this authority the separation of lawmaking and law-preserving violence is suspended" (*ibid.*). This means that potentially – but very often this becomes a sad and tragic actuality – the police can do as they please by means of the right of decree. They can exercise sovereign power, sovereign violence, extending the logic of war and racism to all aspects of daily life. What is understood by 'police' here is of course not (or not simply) the police department, the police officer, and so on, but the logic of security, the right claimed by the State to eliminate external as well as internal threats, to reduce every human activity and every human being to numbers and data, to remove and expel or protect and purify, to impede the formation of free and joyful singularities while building structures of sadness, enforced identities, debt, and death. In other words, it stands for the construction of the biopolitical and thanatopolitical frame – the prison, for Foucault; the camp, for Agamben – within which the machinery of disposability can function at its best. It is the implementation of a system of cruelty resting on racism, suspicion, and resentment (in the Nietzschean sense). Although for Benjamin there is an intimate relation between violence and the law in general, the violence (or the "law") of the police has special characteristics of its own, and it represents, especially in democratic societies, "the greatest conceivable degeneration of violence" (287). Indeed, "it marks the point at which the state . . . can no longer guarantee through the legal system the empirical ends that it desires at any price to attain" (*ibid.*). It is always, Benjamin adds, a question of *security*. Today, it is even more evident than in the past that the security state, the society of control, virtually subsumes all aspects of life under itself. Benjamin gives an excellent and evocative description of the police institution: "Its power is formless, like its nowhere tangible, all-pervasive, ghostly presence in the life of civilized states" (*ibid.*). He also says, in a way that may at first seem paradoxical, that "though the police may, in particulars, everywhere appear the same, it cannot finally be denied that their spirit is less devastating where they represent, in absolute monarchy, the power of a ruler in which legislative and executive supremacy are united, than in democracies where their existence, elevated by no such relation, bears witness [as I have noted above] to the greatest conceivable degeneration of violence" (*ibid.*; brackets added). This is a very important point, especially in liberal societies, and, truly, in the neoliberal world, where the fiction of individual freedom and independence, the fiction of identity, is generally accepted as a sign of social and civil emancipation, but it really indicates the police's own emancipation from the twofold (lawmaking and law-preserving) character of violence and its subsequent degeneration. From this point of view, which is that of the logic of security and control, those who appear as individuals are truly only numbers or data, compulsory identities replace open singularities. The formless and panoptic power of the police implements the politics of number, whose ends are security and order but whose means will have to be cruel, racist, degrading, and inhuman. All this is concealed behind the mantle of democracy, the whining ideologies of nationalism and patriotism, the rhetoric about the importance of defending one's sovereignty and borders for the sake of guaranteeing the functioning of democratic institutions and of increasing their effectiveness. In truth, what one (the One) builds is a society of fear and a culture of servitude. It is certainly not trans-stitutions of joy that are constructed, but destinies of passivity, misery, and sadness. The identity made through servitude and fear, passivity and sadness, impedes the passage to the singularity of the overhuman and common. The stronger the docility and obedience of identity, the less likely will be the rupture, the experience of the threshold. Yet, in a manner similar to Evans and Giroux's suggestion of education and critical pedagogy, as a way of reigniting the imagination, or in other words, recuperating access to the gathering threshold of action and change, Benjamin speaks of language and understanding, "the conference" (289), where precisely there is a gathering, a bringing and coming together, or the *assembly*, in Hardt and Negri's words. For Benjamin, it is a matter of civility – as we will see in Balibar, too – an exit from the logic of the normalization of violence.

When I use the notion of civility, I obviously have in mind the work of Étienne Balibar. However, I think that essentially this notion also addresses Benjamin's otherwise difficult concept of divine, pure, or unalloyed violence. In a sense, I believe that it is useless today to insist too much on interpreting the difference between mythic and divine violence in Benjamin and explaining the latter's 'true' meaning. Interestingly (and, in my view, correctly), Balibar speaks of Benjamin's "striking but obscure formulations" in this respect (Balibar 2015: 104). At the same time, it is possible to suggest that mythic violence relates to what we have been calling, with Evans and Giroux, among others, the normalization of violence and that divine violence – which we refrain from calling "sovereign," as Benjamin does – is in a situation of radical rupture with respect to it; perhaps we can say that it stands on a different ontological plane. Thus, it is more useful to start from the fact that there is violence (political violence) and that this violence, as Balibar notes with a reference to Rosa Luxemburg, has an *"antinomic nature,"* namely, it is "not only the violence exercised by the state but also that employed by the revolution" (*ibid.*; original emphasis). The latter does certainly not correspond to Benjamin's divine, or unalloyed, violence, but, as Balibar points out, it is "present in Hegel and passes from Hegel to Marx and Lenin" (*ibid.*). However, Balibar says that in Luxemburg there is also the introduction of *"another dialectic* (that of violence and antiviolence) into the practice of [radical] transformation itself on the basis of an understanding that political violence can never be completely controlled" (105; brackets added; original emphasis). In the introduction to his book, Balibar says that this problematic of antiviolence is also present, "tendentially at least" (8), in Marx. He then asks the question as to "whether nonviolence is not marked by antinomies just as profound as those associated with violence" (106). He leaves that question open in *Violence and Civility*, but, with a reference to Derrida, suggests the possible existence of "the violence of nonviolence," which would be "a terrible violence" (*ibid.*). Balibar says this in the chapter on "Strategies of Civility," to which I will return. Before doing that, let us understand the general question of the relation of violence and civility. First of all, it is important to note Balibar's problematization of civility as "anti-violence," a "politics of politics" capable of structuring the ground of a rebirth of the political, of political activity (viii–ix). Antiviolence, or civility, is also a transindividual concept, indicating "that no one can be emancipated by others but, as well, that no one can emancipate herself without others" (6). Balibar calls this situation, or relation of relations, *equaliberty* (viii and 6). The underlining concept to equaliberty, he says in the preface, is "a *becoming citizen of the subject* (qua counterpart of the sovereign) and a *becoming subject* (in the moral, juridical, social sense) *of the citizen*" (viii; original emphasis). As Jason Read says dealing with Balibar in his book on the politics of transindividuality, "Equaliberty is the name, or concept, that defines the citizen as a transindividual individuality" (Read 2016: 96). Read says, "The citizen of equaliberty is the insurrectionary side to political identity" (*ibid.*). As such, "it cuts through the division between individual and society, public and private" (*ibid.*). This is in keeping with Balibar's own definition of equaliberty. However, Read has a critical take on Balibar's concept. He agrees that equaliberty is "a transindividual condition, passing through the collective recognition of the rights of the individual" (*ibid.*). Yet, he adds, "that does not mean that it is lived collectivity" (*ibid.*). There is, he says, "an unmistakable overlap between transindividuality and equaliberty" (95), but they are not the same concept, or figure, nor are they developed "on the same philosophical terrain" (*ibid.*). The problem seems to be that in the subject/citizen of equaliberty one still needs recognition, and, in a sense, one remains too close to the model of intersubjectivity and the general paradigm of the subject. It is in this sense that, with a reference to Foucault, Balibar also addresses the equally important question of the way in which subjectivities oscillate between subjection and subjectivation (Balibar 2015: viii). All this calls forth a multiplicity of strategies of civility, as we will see. In what follows, I will bear in mind the idea of the plurality of strategies of antiviolence. As for the question of subjectivity and of becoming subject, I have repeatedly said that I am proposing the abandonment of these notions, as they belong to the same metaphysics of subjectivity and subjection that must be overcome, and a passage to the (unalloyed, if I may here make an allusion to Benjamin) concept of singularities as well as to the concept of the gathering threshold (the assemblage) of trans-dividuality. I have repeatedly said that I am not convinced that subjectivation can be an exit from subjection, but rather an element in the same metaphysics or paradigm, and that we need a new dialectic and a new ontology, or better a movement (or a plurality of movements) of re-assemblage and re-composition, the capacity to recognize and valorize the de-disindividuating power of the gathering thresholds, without turning all this into yet another subject. In this sense, Benjamin's obscurity, as he posits an unalloyed plane of ontological power (which he calls "divine violence"), or his notion of a *real state of emergency*, can be useful again (Benjamin 1968: 257). Indeed, what is at stake with the concept of singularity is not at all the fact of becoming subject, but rather the open and plural process of becoming itself. Again, it is not a matter of being individuated, but rather of enduring the individuating process, which must remain incomplete. It might be objected that a measure of individuation and subjection is inevitable and that subjectivation is the best we can have. In other words, it might be objected that a notion of singularity as fully outside the paradigm of subjectivity (including the option of subjectivation) is simply utopian. However, besides the fact that we are increasingly in need of a utopian orientation, singularities are concrete utopias, as I hope to indicate in the course of this writing. To settle for subjectivation, as an exit from subjection, risks being a form of capitulation to fear and servitude, to the diktat of identity, or better, identification, namely, to the logic of the police. It would be the same as the joyful obedience described by Lordon and the illusion of freedom typical of many people in western democracies. The utopian orientation is, to the contrary, one of the strategies against the prospect of infinitely extending the oppressive reality of the present, of fear, servitude, and compulsory identification. This is what a singular rupture with the logic of number is: to think beyond the metaphysics of subjectivity necessarily accompanied by the prison and the police, debt and death, the permanent exception and the normalization of violence, co-linearization and disindividuation. The prospect of civility, or antiviolence, means emancipation from the police at all levels, an exit from the capture of number, and, as Fanon suggests, the construction of a new humanity.

The importance of the concept of civility, or antiviolence, becomes particularly evident in relation to the reality of the border and the question of migration. It might be first of all useful to stress that, as Balibar says, the border is no longer simply at the border; the politics of the border and migration has a global and local dimension at the same time, and it virtually shapes all aspects of daily life everywhere. What most essentially characterizes this reality has already been mentioned above in the notions of racism and disposability. Both notions point out dimensions of extreme violence for which Balibar uses the word *cruelty*. Just like in the discussion of Foucault's notion of racism above, the targets of these biopolitical forms of extreme violence are both the external and internal other, the annihilation of the human by means of the police (broadly and narrowly construed). Balibar suggests an analytical distinction between *ultraobjective* and *ultrasubjective* cruelty. Both forms pursue the "elimination of humanity and the human in man" (Balibar 2015: 52) – an impossible task, yet capable of bringing about incredible suffering and misery. Ultraobjective cruelty "calls for treating masses of human beings as things or useless remnants, while [ultrasubjective cruelty] requires that individuals and groups be represented as incarnations of evil, diabolical powers that threaten the subject from within and have to be eliminated at all costs, up to and including self-destruction" (*ibid.*; brackets added). A quick glance at forms of exchange among users on social media gives a precise measure of the accuracy of this description and of how this culture of cruelty (grounded in fear and ignorance) has become all-pervasive. But this is only a sinister reflection of a more systemic and structured drive of biopolitical power, the machinery of exclusion, disposability, and social death, as well as the production of a distorted (and racist) desire of identity, security, and a misplaced idea of happiness. For Balibar, the term *racism* is "something like the metonymic name of this problematic unity," namely, the unity of these two forms (ultraobjective and ultrasubjective) of extermination (53). They both posit themselves beyond the exception, and thus become normalized, as is the case in a situation of permanent war. Their basic principle is to relegate individuals and "entire populations to spaces of invisibility and disposability" (Evans and Giroux 2015: 140). This is not only the case in dictatorships or openly authoritarian regimes. The action of the police (this time especially in the strict and technical sense of law enforcement), particularly against African-Americans and other minority groups, in the United States is a perfect illustration of this. It represents what Benjamin has called "the greatest conceivable degeneration of violence" (1978: 278) in a society that wears the mask of democracy and freedom; it also gives a measure of the biopolitical mode of *cruelty* in the problematic sense suggested by Balibar. The police (both in its strict and broad sense) represent the quintessence of racism, in the sense we have seen in Fanon and Foucault, and of the biopolitics of cruelty in its ultraobjective and ultrasubjective modes. Indeed, the overwhelming and conspicuous presence of the police in a society, such as is the case in the United States, is not a guarantee for the reduction of violence, but rather for its production and intensification. As Alex Vitale says in *The End of Policing*, there is continuity between colonial and modern policing in the U.S. Just like in the past, the police today also "enforce a system of laws designed to reproduce and maintain economic inequality, usually along racialized lines" (2017: 52). He also says that "when individuals and communities look to the police to solve their problem they are in essence mobilizing the machinery of their own oppression" (53). Interestingly, in his book that deals with various aspects of policing, from policing sex work and the war on drugs to the militarization of schools, the criminalization of homelessness, the repression of political movements, and so on, Vitale also has a chapter by the title (taken from a news report) "We Called for Help, and they Killed My Son," which is about the criminalization and outright execution of people with mental illness or disabilities, but which also reveals the hidden texture of a society in which cruelty has replaced civility, the principle of human disposability has more currency than that of human dignity, and the swift neutralization of the other, the foreign, the enemy has precedence over understanding and care. The argument can be made that the spectacular violence we often see in terms of mass shootings, especially those lacking an explicit political motive (and thus appearing more senseless), is a direct consequence of the machinery of police control and police violence. It is often a mere extension of the institutional and biopolitical purpose of "managing the poor and non-white" (53) as well as other minority groups, whose enforced (yet often disaffected and explosive) identity threatens the stability of the stale, dominant One. Criminalization then becomes a method for social and biopolitical control. One of the main theses in Michelle Alexander's *The New Jim Crow* (2012) precisely states as much, and it implicitly recasts Foucault's notion of *modern racism* as *colorblindness*, which is perhaps a more refined biopolitical notion. Alexander says, "In the era of colorblindness, it is no longer permissible to use race, explicitly, as a justification for discrimination, exclusion, and social contempt. So we don't. Rather than rely on race, we use our criminal justice system to label people of color 'criminals' and then engage in all practices we supposedly left behind. Today it is perfectly legal to discriminate against criminals in nearly all the ways it was once legal to discriminate against African Americans" (2). Institutional violence of an extreme type, *cruelty*, is thus inscribed within the criminal justice system, the logic of the police, in ways that purportedly take distance from the ideological excesses of the past, but in fact reproduce them in a more subtle and effective fashion. To be (potentially or actually) criminalized are all identities that, as Balibar says, are "regarded as non-identities" (2002: 77). They are stigmatized as different, other, foreign; they are the enemy. Obviously, the distorted and cruel construction of the other, the enemy, is not an exclusively American phenomenon. In fact, it is something that takes place all over the world. Even the category of colorblindness, or any similar technical and apparently neutral category of the logic of the police, is rather widespread and common and applicable to many places. What is illustrative of the United States is the intensity of policing and its (apparently paradoxical) effect on the intensification of violence, mass incarceration, and the prison industrial complex. Behind the façade of colorblindness, racism, as Angela Davis says in *Are Prisons Obsolete?*, "surreptitiously defines social and economic structures in ways that are difficult to identify and thus are much more damaging" (2003: 38). The same point made by Vitale in Chapter Three of his book, "The School-to-Prison Pipeline" (2017: 55–75) is made by Davis who speaks about "the damage wrought by the expansion of the prison system in the schools located in poor communities of color that replicate the structures and regimes of the prison" (2003: 38). And she continues, "When children attend schools that place a greater value on discipline and security than on knowledge and intellectual development, they are attending prep schools for prison" (38–39). The "punitive disciplinary systems" of neoliberal schools, as Vitale says (2017: 57), as well as the general machinery of police surveillance and control in the schools and in the cities, intensifies the politics and culture of cruelty and disindividuation, whose horizon remain the prison (and for many people there is a prison before the prison and one after it), the camp, poverty (debt), and extermination (social or actual death).

The question of extreme violence (cruelty) and the biopolitical drive toward extermination (exterminism) is also the subject of Bertrand Ogilvie's volume, *L'homme jetable* (*Disposable Man*) (2012).[1] First of all, very relevant to this book, Ogilvie addresses the question of identity, or rather, identification, as inscribed in "a process of relative individuation" (47). As such, all we have is "the indefinite and asymptotic pursuit of an uncertain identification" (*ibid.*). This is very close to one of the main theses of this book, touching both on the openness of what I have called the gathering threshold and of singularity. Violence already emerges in the forceful reduction of this openness to a closed and stigmatized identity and of singularities to numbers and data (passed on as individuals). But there is in Ogilvie that same antinomic notion of violence we have seen problematized by Balibar. To be sure, Ogilvie says that there is nothing "natural or original in violence: to the contrary, it is a product, a result" (48). And he speaks of "procedures of fabrication" of violence (*ibid.*). He repeats the same concept, saying that "violence is not 'something,' a source or principle, but always a result" (53). I believe that this must be understood in the same way in which for Simondon there is no *principle* of individuation, namely, 'something' that remains behind or before individuation, but the individuating process itself, the *process* of individuation. Thus, violence would always be a result of such a process, accompanying it indefinitely as a result at each stage of its unfolding, but varying in intensity and orientation, as "there is no degree zero of violence" (54). It can go from the "insensitive to the intolerable, but also from the physical to the political" (*ibid.*). What is interesting is that these variations "produce effects of servitude or emancipation" (*ibid.*). In a sense, we find again the antinomic nature of violence, but this time in a dialectical movement that recalls some figures of Presocratic thinking, such as Anaximenes (with the density and rarity of air), Heraclitus, and Empedocles (with the forces of love and strife, attraction and repulsion). But this movement due to the variations of intensity and orientation of violence can also be understood in terms of affective power or force in the Spinozian sense of the increase or decrease of such power (*potentia*) with the respective resulting emotions of joy and sadness. Thus, so far it seems to be more a matter of potency than of violence commonly understood. Ogilvie shows that by saying that violence is "force, potency, vigor, but also the excess of this force, its abusive usage with respect to the norm of judgment" (75). Indeed, the problematization of violence as violence (i.e., as abusive use of force) begins, in Ogilvie, with the passage to *modern and contemporary violence*, which is "a new [*inédite*] configuration of violence" (55), whose most important trait is that it is "not only violence in politics, but violence-of-politics" [non pas seulement violence dans la politique, mais violence-de-la-politique] (*ibid.*). This new configuration of violence is "violence without address" [une violence sans adresse] (60 and 81), namely, a type of violence which is no longer transgressive, but normalized and structured. As Louis Carré says in a review of Ogilvie's book, this form of violence is *sans adresse* "insofar as it submits subjects to an anonymous, quasi-objective process of dehumanization that returns them to their 'radical in-significance' [Ogilvie 2012: 77]" (Carré 2013: 2).[2] "As such, it participates" (*ibid.*), Carré continues quoting Ogilvie, in "the production of disposable-man" (Ogilvie 2012: 74). Essentially, we are on the terrain of biopolitics, a term Ogilvie mentions later as he deals with Foucault (133), and bare life.

It is a matter of bare life in the deepest ontological sense, for it involves not simply the ban, abandonment, and exposure to the vulnerable (in themselves already cruel enough), but the extermination or total annihilation of the very conditions of existence and being-with. For Ogilvie, with extreme violence, "the modern subject is confronted, more than with its own destruction, with its impossibility, more precisely the possibility of its impossibility" (77). It is not a situation in which, by means of a dialectical movement in which one stakes one's own life (as Hegel says), a reversal of power relations becomes possible, for that still requires recognition. Thus, it is not even the fear of death, not even facing the danger, that can reestablish conditions of existence – let alone the dignity of the good life, happiness, and the good death. With extreme violence, Ogilvie continues, the modern subject is confronted "not only with its individual death but with the discovery that its life might not have value for anyone, and from there, quickly, to the negation of the very possibility of its structure" (*ibid.*). This concrete dystopia actually represents the unfolding of the history of sovereignties, the history of conquest and modern colonial expansion with its many occurrences of genocidal exterminations (78). But, says Ogilvie, it is also present in "the most ordinary and microscopic phenomena of so-called private life (in reality so public!) that characterize the formation of modern salaried populations" (*ibid.*). Even more so in the insecurity experienced, in the age of security, by the precariat, the contingency of contemporary life and labor. Indeed, the current obsession with security is one of the clearest signs of cruelty, as it displaces vast sections of the world population in situations of utter insecurity proximate to the reality of extermination. This is what I call *the politics of number*, which is not only the reduction of people (singularities) to numbers, but the very extermination of the singular, the plurality of singularity, in its physical and/or political structuring possibility and mode. In the words of Ogilvie, the logic of cruelty and exterminism involves the systemic idea that one can "treat humans, 'human resources,' like things: manage them, organize them in 'networks,' control their 'circulation' within a geometric space, like mechanical forces, electrical currents or 'flow'" (81). This violence *sans adresse* is both gratuitous and extremely rational, both indistinct and deeply structured/structural.

At the end of his chapter on strategies of civility, or antiviolence, Balibar agrees that "the central question is still that of the concept of identification and its other face, disidentification" (2015: 126), and, it may be added, individuation and disindividuation. He says this with some important references to the work of Deleuze and Guattari and that of Foucault. In Deleuze and Foucault, these strategies have "an avowed Nietzschean reference to *play*" (*ibid.*). In Foucault, this is especially evident in his idea of "an aesthetics of existence or care of the self" (124), the invention of one's own life as a work of art, the production of the self. In Deleuze (and Guattari), there is also a strong Spinozian moment of "active-passive" disidentification (126), able "to yield a radically different 'ontology'" (125). Balibar calls this a "practical philosophy of passivity (or the fiction of passivity)" that opens up a "transindividual space of 'desire,'" where "the fixity and unity of the 'self'" can be dissolved and a fluid exchange, perhaps a con-fusion, between the "self" and the "other" can take place (126). This can also be related to the discussion of Taoist passivity we saw in Chapter One and to the idea of the gathering threshold present throughout this book. What essentially challenges the central question of identification and disidentification is "the play of identities or of the proliferation of masks," which Balibar says, provides "a radical opposition to normality and normalization which, by definition, exclude play of any sort" (126). However, Balibar stresses, the dissolution of the self, or subject, the deterritorialization made possible by "the Deleuzian 'machinic assemblages of desire'" (123), requires *caution*, as Deleuze and Guattari say in *A Thousand Plateaus* (1987: 150; Balibar 2015: 124). Indeed, Balibar continues, "it must be granted that the dissolution of the subject is a double-edged sword" (*ibid.*). He says that "Deleuze and Guattari are well aware of the danger; that is doubtless why they so often evoke the need to be careful with deterritorialization . . . and the 'principle of caution,' as a crucial aspect of politics" (*ibid.*). Yet, once this caution is exercised and the danger of falling into new forms of ultraobjective or ultrasubjective violence is avoided, the liberation from the servitude of compulsory identity, or identification, hence the liberation from the fear of *becoming nothing*, or better, *no one*, but many, the plurality of singularity, can perhaps yield a promise of increased potency, namely, of joy. Strategies of civility or antiviolence may be laborious and demanding, but they can perhaps open the ontology of the singular, of singularities beyond/without number, beyond the paradigm of individuality and the metaphysics of the subject. Perhaps this is also what Benjamin's *divine violence*, "which is lethal without spilling blood" (1978: 297), points to: a radically alternative ontological plane. This might be the plane for the construction of a new humanity, as Fanon says. It is not an elevation of violence, but emancipation from it. What so often changes to violence proper (as a form of abuse) stays as the vacillation of the perfection of potency, which includes the power-to of civility and care. On the last page of *Willing Slaves of Capital*, with a reference to Spinoza, Frédéric Lordon says that the common life, guided by reason, "is not a choice that people are free to reject" (2014: 162). Yet, "the relations that govern the organisation of this common life are neither written in advance nor given for all eternity, and it is thus permitted to prefer some over others" (*ibid.*). For Spinoza, the guidance of reason is the condition for freedom and happiness, which are denied to many through fear and violence, disposability and the threat (or the actuality) of extermination. Yet, when reason, namely, civility and care, guides the many, the multitude, and their power increases, the destructive machinery of cruelty and death can be deactivated, the logic of disposability overcome and discarded. As Spinoza says in *Political Treatise* (III, 6), "sound reason cannot require that each man should remain in control of his own right," and "the more a man is guided by reason . . . , the more he is free" (2000: 50). The common life is then asserted in an anti-individualistic and trans-dividual fashion. Singularities are not individuals in control of their own right, but assemblages of potency and confidence, an alternative to any form of cruelty, and an expression of what Spinoza calls *piety* (*pietas*), namely, the "desire to do good" deriving from the guidance of reason (1992: 174; *Ethics* IV, Pr 37, Scholium 1).

NOTES

1. The translation of Ogilvie's passages is my own.
2. The translation of Carré's passages is my own.

SIX

Capture and Thresholds

The Politics of Number, the Accidental Glass

The concept of *threshold* is very important in Gilles Deleuze and Félix Guattari's *A Thousand Plateaus* (1987). Particularly interesting for us is the idea that "the self is only a threshold, a door, a becoming between two multiplicities" (249). We have already seen in Chapter One, above, the intimate relationship between the threshold and the door. Thresholds and doors are, in the course of a journey, sites "where becoming itself becomes" (*ibid.*). They are a sort of *transduction* (Simondon's concept) with all its *internal resonance* (Simondon's concept, again), a crossing and a lingering, a whispering (or a shouting) and a hearing, "*a multiplicity transforming itself into a string of other multiplicities*" (*ibid.*). It is in this sense that we have insisted on the concept (and metaphor) of a gathering threshold. Perhaps what should also be mentioned is that the use of the 'we' pronoun here is not at all a reference to the sovereign *pluralis majestatis* (for sovereignty is finished), but to the plural of multiplicity, singularity, and trans-dividuality. What Deleuze and Guattari call rhizome, or multiplicities, whose outside (or grid) is the linear *plane of consistency*, is certainly not "the One," nor is it simply "the multiple," as the result of an addition to the One; in other words, as we will soon see, it is not the denumerable, but the nondenumerable. They say, "It is not the One that becomes Two or even directly three, four, five, etc. It is not a multiple derived from the One, or to which One is added $(n + 1)$" (21). It is "always a middle (*milieu*)" (*ibid.*), and, as such, a threshold. They continue, "It constitutes linear multiplicities with n dimensions having neither subject nor object, which can be laid out on a plane of consistency, and from which the One is always subtracted $(n - 1)$" (*ibid.*). This is what I am (we are) calling singularities, but this is also very important for a framing of the concept of the politics of number, which insists on reducing singularities to what they are not and cannot be. Singularities cannot (ultimately) be reduced to numbers – as much as the system, the State, ("the axiomatic of capital," for Deleuze and Guattari), try to do so—because the threshold of deterritotialization, or the line of flight, the infinitizing moment, extends itself to the plane of consistency, which is the specific *"field of immanence* of desire" (154), covering it up (11), transductively amplifying the resonance between the molar and the molecular (60), "becoming-molecular" (473), that is, insurgent, revolutionary assemblages.

Singularities: To say this in the spirit of Laozi and Daoist philosophy, the singular has no character of its own. It takes as its own the character of the common. Singularities are thus multiplicities, pluralities, rhizomatic occurrences, "deterritotialized intensities" (32), migrations, and, again, thresholds. They are also *becomings, nomadic essences, haecceities* (507), and what Deleuze and Guattari call 'bodies without organs.' But the word 'haecceity' needs to be remarked upon. As Deleuze and Guattari point out in an interesting endnote, 'haecceity' is "sometimes written 'ecceity,' deriving the word from *ecce*, 'here is.' This is an error, since Duns Scotus created the word and the concept from *haec*, 'this thing.' But it is a fruitful error because it suggests a mode of individuation that is distinct from that of a thing or a subject" (540–541, endnote 33). Indeed, moving beyond the subject, or the thing, this mode of individuation points to the process of becoming as such, the becoming of becoming, and thus to the open, unfinished (and unfinishable), impossible individuation. This does not alter the concrete character of singularities; rather, it strengthens it. Singularities are neither individuals nor subjects or things. They are gathering thresholds, flows, and instances/intensities of being-here (or being-there), which constantly surpass themselves, cross over new thresholds according to an infinitizing desire, "a desire of eternity," as Simondon says. But, he adds, a desire is a reality, "the emergence of a dynamism of being" (2013: 275), which produces transindividuality, or trans-dividual assemblages. Another way of looking at this is to say, with Heidegger (notably, according to his commentary on the archaic forms for "being" and "beings" in Ancient Greek: respectively, ἐόν and ἐόντα, in "The Anaximander Fragment"), that singularities, "the gathering that clears and shelters," include all absence in what is present (1975: 37). To be sure, he says that it is the singular form ἐόν ("being"), in particular, that "indicates what is singular as such, what is singular in its numerical unity and what is singularly and unifyingly one before all number" (33). Yet what Heidegger is saying is that what is "before all number," the singular, precisely, is not denumerable (we will go back to this concept with Deleuze and Guattari), and thus it is truly less or more than one – certainly not one in its usual sense. The inclusion of the absent in the present, in presence, "remains ambiguous" (35), or, to use a concept by Simondon, *metastable*. The unifying movement is rhizomatic in character, producing a being-here (or being-there) equal to "the field of immanence of desire, the plane of consistency" (Deleuze and Guattari 1987: 154), thus a line of flight, which is "the most difficult of all" (202), the passing of the limit, the production of new waves and new thresholds. What is "singular in its numerical unity" (Heidegger), the nondenumerable, opens up not to the seriality of individual beings, but to the constitutive plurality of the singular as such, to singularities.

The chapter of *A Thousand Plateaus* that will occupy us more here is Chapter 13, on apparatuses of capture, political sovereignty, the axiomatic of capital, the town and the State as "different thresholds of consistency" (432), and, especially, the denumerable and nondenumerable sets. The town, "the correlate of the road," is defined by Deleuze and Guattari as "a phenomenon of *transconsistency*, a *network*, because it is fundamentally in contact with other towns" (432). They also say that the town "represents a threshold of deterritorialization, because whatever the material involved, it must be deterritorialized enough to enter the network" (*ibid.*). The type of power of the town "has egalitarian pretensions, regardless of the form it takes: tyrannical, democratic, oligarchic, aristocratic" (*ibid.*). The State, on the other hand, "is a phenomenon of *intraconsistency*" (433). Differently from the horizontal lines characterizing the polarization of the town, the State, which "makes the town resonate with the countryside" (*ibid.*), "operates by stratification; in other words, it forms a vertical, hierarchized aggregate that spans the horizontal lines in a dimension of depth" (*ibid.*). Essentially, "the central power of the State is hierarchical" (*ibid.*), for its center is not in the middle, as is the case with the town, but on top, and it operates "through subordination" (*ibid.*). It is in this sense that the form of apparatus of capture specifically defines State societies (435). I have briefly mentioned urban societies and their mode of polarization, but I here gloss over other forms of societies dealt with by Deleuze and Guattari, such as nomadic societies. What I want to point out, as an introduction to the issue of capture, the axiomatic of capital and State violence, *machinic enslavement* (*subjugation*) and *social subjection*, is the conceptual difference drawn by Deleuze and Guattari between the "limit" and the "threshold." For them, "the limit designates the penultimate marking a necessary rebeginning, and the threshold the ultimate marking an inevitable change" (438). Essentially, "beyond the limit there lies a threshold" (*ibid.*). This is also relevant to some recent works on the question of the border, which precisely problematize the difference between the border and the limit, or frontier (see Mezzadra and Neilson 2013; Balibar 2002). Here becomes apparent that the traditional, sovereigntist view of the border as a limit, a frontier, does not correspond to reality and that the border should be understood as a threshold of deterritorialization, a line of flight – "(a new assemblage)" (Deleuze and Guattari 1987: 439). Deleuze and Guattari also say that the threshold, which comes "after" the limit (they put "after" in quotes), "is in fact already there" – though "at a distance" (440). In a sense, it is like a concrete utopia, or heterotopia – already there, "but outside the limit" (*ibid.*). The point is, then, to explode and dissolve the limit.

The limit is especially that of the State and State violence. Yet the State explodes and dissolves with its limit(s), and this is the doing, not necessarily of revolutionary action, but of the capitalist axiomatic itself, as it becomes (or is already by default) global. Speaking about violence (as well as the nakedness of labor and the independence/sovereignty of capital), Deleuze and Guattari point out that *"State policing or lawful violence . . . consists in capturing while simultaneously constituting a right to capture. It is an incorporated, structural violence distinct from every kind of direct violence"* (448). Against all evidence, the State will claim that its violence is a mere reaction to the "primal" violence of "criminals . . . primitives . . . nomads," and so on (*ibid.*), exercised "in order that peace may reign" (*ibid.*). In truth, what we usually call 'politics' (the politics of States) is but a form of organized crime. This is why, as Balibar (2015) suggests, we need a regrounding of the conditions of possibility of the political. But this regrounding, the contingency of struggle, as Sandro Mezzadra and Brett Neilson say in *The Politics of Operations* (2019), is beyond the State (yet against it), perhaps at the multiplicity of its deterritorialized thresholds, as is evidenced by the actions of various NGOs around the issue of migration in the Mediterranean, to give a notable example. What Deleuze and Guattari wrote decades ago, that "capitalism develops an economic order that could do without the State" (1987: 454), becomes increasingly true today. But, even politically, the State has become obsolete: its sovereignty, just like the unity and independence of the individual, or the function of the police, only reveals an extreme degree of capture: machinic enslavement and social subjection. In the former case, the human being is a component of the machine; in the latter, a subjected *user*, "not enslaved by the technical machine but rather subjected to it" (457). We have seen in a previous chapter how these two modalities (machinic enslavement, or subjugation, and social subjection) come together in the nakedness of debt, algorithmic control, and social death. The illusion of subjectivation (or subjectification), an apparent exit from social subjection, is part of the ideology of the independent and sovereign individual. Indeed, as we have repeatedly said, subjectivation is part of the subject paradigm and thus only an offshoot of subjection, not really a radical rupture with it, or an alternative to it. There is, as Deleuze and Guattari point out, a correspondence between subjectivation and subjection. They are both modalities of the apparatus of capture of the State. The former is perhaps more pernicious than the latter, for it seems to forget the sadness of subjection (and subjugation) and embrace the easy joy of a false freedom – a wishful thinking and joyful obedience. It is, as Deleuze and Guattari say, a "magical capture" (460). The illusion of subjectivation is inscribed in the form of the contract, thus in liberal (and neoliberal) ideology. Indeed, as they say, the contract (the seemingly nonviolent limit of State violence) "appears as the proceeding of subjectification, the outcome of which is subjection" (*ibid.*). The contract form is "finally, the Subject that binds itself" (*ibid.*), the utmost of self-deception and passionate servitude, which is what "magical capture" means.

Minorities: Singularities are minorities. Deleuze and Guattari say that a minority "can be small in number; but it can also be the largest in number, constitute an absolute, indefinite majority" (469). Minorities, just like singularities, are the opposite of number, their antagonistic other. What distinguishes a minority from a majority, both of which "can be numerous, or even infinite" (*ibid.*), is "the relation internal to the number" (470). Essentially, the majority is defined by a denumerable set, "whereas the minority is defined as a nondenumerable set, however many elements it may have" (*ibid.*). The difference between the denumerable and nondenumerable set has nothing to do with the quantity of elements contained, but rather with "the *connection*, the 'and' produced between elements" (*ibid.*) or sets, the line of flight, the open threshold of trans-dividuality. The nondenumerable, the singular, is outside the axiomatic paradigm, outside the paradigm of capture, in a constant process of "escape and flux" (*ibid.*). As Deleuze and Guattari say, "What is proper to the minority is to assert a power of the nondenumerable, even if that minority is composed of a single member" (*ibid.*). In Chapter 11 of *Deleuze and Ethics*, "Ethics between Particularity and Universality," Audronė Žukauskaitė says, "The specific feature defining becoming-minoritarian and minorities as such is related to the notion of multiplicity. Deleuze and Guattari assert that the difference between minorities and the majority is not a difference in number but a difference between denumerable and nondenumerable units" (Žukauskaitė 2011: 194–195). She continues, "The key idea is that the majority is composed of denumerable or quantitative elements, while minorities are defined by non-denumerable or qualitative elements, which cannot be counted or integrated into the axiomatic logic of capitalism" (195). This is precisely what we are seeking: not subjectivities and their corresponding shadows of subjection, but open and dangerous (because *in danger*) singularities, which cannot be counted, the neither/nor of *whatever* being, *whatever* becoming, as we saw in Chapter Four, above. This is what Deleuze and Guattari call "the becoming-minoritarian of everybody" (105), which is what all becoming is, for "majority is never becoming" (106). A majority is a stifled and stagnant, amorphous reality. Minority, on the other hand, means multiplicities. Deleuze and Guattari powerfully say, "Woman: we all have to become that, whether we are male or female. Non-white: we all have to become that, whether we are white, yellow, or black" (470). As Guillaume Sibertin-Blanc says, "The becoming-minoritarian work simultaneously against the empty universal of the hegemonic norm and against the inclusive-excluding particularization of the minority as sub-system" (2016:

235). The point is not building a politics of identity. To the contrary, the point is destroying all identity (or at least calling it into question). Becoming is "necessarily *singular* and not 'individual'" (237). The politics of identity, the "response of the States, or of the axiomatic . . . consists in translating the minorities into denumerable sets or subsets, which would enter as elements into the majority, which could be counted among the majority" (Deleuze and Guattari 1987: 470). However, the point is to *prefer not to* be counted (Bartleby), not to be dominated (Machiavelli). Indeed, minorities, the nondenumerable, "would receive no adequate expression by becoming elements of the majority, in other words, by becoming a denumerable finite set" (*ibid.*). As Žukauskaitė says, "the majority is always supported by the state and other structures of power" (2011: 195) precisely because it is "compatible with the axiomatic logic of capitalism, which transforms every heterogeneous element into the flow of homogeneous quantities" (*ibid.*). But minorities "carry within them a deeper movement that challenges the worldwide axiomatic" (Deleuze and Guattari 1987: 472). They are against the State-form, and "the State-form is not appropriate to them" (*ibid*); they are against identity, for identity is nothing but a phenomenon of capture. In their explosive book, Deleuze and Guattari speak of minorities as intending to smash capitalism and become a war machine – against the institutional war machine – capable of bringing about a new idea of communism, a new threshold of the singular and common, the nondenumerable multiplication of molecular assemblages and revolutionary networks.

Thresholds: As Stavros Stavrides says in *Towards the City of Thresholds* (2019), "Thresholds mark areas of potential change" (xviii). They are "in-between spaces and times" (2), "[f]ragments of a different life" (*ibid.*) where encounters with otherness become actual. They signal the limits of identities and their crossing into otherness, new identities, which, however, to use Simondon's language, remain metastable, or unstable and incomplete. Indeed, as Stavrides says, the "wisdom hidden in the threshold experience lies in the awareness that otherness can only be approached by opening the borders of identity" (9). Interestingly, Stavrides calls "civility" a moment in "an art of building thresholds between people or social groups" (10). One is reminded of Leibniz's notion that the "place of others is the true point of perspective in politics as in morality" (1972: 81). For Leibniz that has to do with happiness, love, and equity – perhaps another way of speaking of civility. A reference should also be made to Balibar's notion of civility as antiviolence, which we have seen in the previous chapter. Perhaps we can now better understand that antiviolence itself is grounded in the ability to "become other," as Stavrides says (2019: 10). He says, beautifully, "One departs from themselves to be an other" (*ibid.*). One crosses a threshold as well as becomes one. Indeed, as Stavrides says, "thresholds mark processes of transformations of social identity," and he stresses that this is "one of the most critical points" of his book (12). Thresholds – and this goes beyond the city, though it may find in the city its best context or illustration – are always lines of flight, as Deleuze and Guattari say, exits or escapes from capture. Capture appears here as the urban enclave, which seen from the outside, Stavrides says, can have a twofold meaning: "it can be either fatal trap (if this enclave takes the form of the camp) or a zone of protection (if this enclave takes the form of a secluded area of privilege)" (35), the gated community. By critically engaging Agamben's notion of exception, Stavrides argues that it is important to grasp it not as "a state," but as "a dynamic mechanism" (38). The camp, he says, is "a model enclave of normalized exception" (37), obviously a situation of total institutionalization and capture. To the contrary, and with a reference to Walter Benjamin's "real state of emergency" (Benjamin 1968: 257), Stavrides says that the threshold, as a dynamic figure of exception, a *mechanism* of exception, "triggers a transformative disruption of normality" (2019: 39).

The concept of threshold is increasingly receiving attention, and it is perhaps one of the most fruitful/powerful notions able to challenge the apparent impasse within social and political life and address the concrete possibilities of social transformation. Seen from the viewpoint of transindividuality, or better, trans-dividuality, thresholds can also be conceived as relations without a subject, thus as what replaces the individual or subject. They are, as Stavrides emphasizes, mechanisms (of exception), not states. Byung-Chul Han also deals with thresholds in *The Expulsion of the Other* (2018). To begin with, Han problematizes the 'disappearance' of the Other and the pathological "proliferation of the Same" (1) – indeed, the "terror of the Same" (3). This is an assertion about the impossible crossing into the other, becoming other. Thresholds do come back through the anxiety engendered by the depressive (rather than repressive) dominance of the Same. Yet, this is a crossing into the vacuity and violence of the Same, a threshold to nothingness. Only the rediscovery of "the *time of the Other*" (77) can provide a change of direction towards the creation of communities (78). But this rediscovery starts from the destruction of the Same, the deconstruction and disposal of one's own identity, understood as fictitious. For Stavrides, the ability to change identity is also the possibility to "visit otherness" (2019: 45), and thus *inhabit thresholds*, where the gathering takes place – gathering, that is, "encounters with otherness" (46).

In the chapter on Walter Benjamin's thresholds, Stavrides addresses the question of discontinuities with the past, ruptures, and the possibility of a liberating future. There is a critique of the private individual, who "builds a shelter for his individuality" (78). The dialectic of trace and aura, the potentialities of past and present, near and distant, shows the presence of thresholds, which "unite those areas that differences tend to keep apart" (87). The figure characterized by this dialectic is the *flâneur*, the opposite of the private individual, who "leaves no traces in the public space" (76). The flâneur, in fact, a figure of trans-dividuality, "searches for traces that will reveal individual trajectories in public space" (82). Perhaps we should understand these "individual trajectories" as fragments, dividualities, and thus what is gathered by the flâneur is a trans-dividual assemblage of directions and traces, "vehicles of aura" (79). Indeed, Stavrides himself says that "the flâneur discovers in the depth of [the] transitoriness [of modern life] traces of an ephemeral, anonymous – if this is not a contradiction in terms – individuality" (*ibid.*). Perhaps the contradiction is avoided – if one needed to avoid contradictions – by understanding precisely 'individuality' as trans-dividuality. The private individual remains submerged and hidden in their fictitious individuality. The flâneur, on the other hand, slips into the dangerous territory of thresholds, in "an attitude of auratic appreciation" (83), *becoming the threshold*. This is a passage to the other, to art, and to the potentiality of a liberated future. To the flâneur, Stavrides says, the ordinary becomes strange. There is here a process of defamiliarization, meant "to expose alienation as a general characteristic of city life" (84). The threshold, a "fleeting moment of sudden revelation" (86) and a line of flight from the ordinary and captured, estranges and defamiliarizes. The dialectics of trace and aura, "crystallized in the concept of threshold" (88), expresses, Stavrides says, "the dynamics of temporal and spatial discontinuity" (*ibid.*). And finally he says that "the flâneur embodies the ambiguous power of thresholds" (*ibid.*). This has to do with the fact that the flâneur is "a man uprooted" (Benjamin 895) and thus "a counterpart of the 'crowd'" (*ibid.*). What is important for us here is that the flâneur, who is not a man of the crowd (Benjamin 1968a: 172), is a threshold figure, a figure of trans-dividuality, and as such an exit from the logic of number. For Stavrides, the flâneur "invents points of rupture in urban space: passages and thresholds" and thus "experiences the city as fragmented and dispersed" (2019: 88). Together with the flâneur, Stavrides reviews another important notion in Benjamin's work, that of glass, which "exposes, bringing the interior very close to the exterior" (90). Glass is "a precarious threshold" (91), and thus perhaps the threshold par excellence.

As "a precarious threshold," glass also points to the contingent and accidental. It is a passage to heterotopias, Foucault's concept that Stavrides takes up in Chapter Six of his book. Stavrides says that heterotopias are "born as places of discontinuity, cracks in the molding" (152). We should keep in mind Stavrides' insistence on understanding the threshold as a mechanism of exception and thus always a moment of rupture. Its dynamic nature and its movement of discontinuity are important here. Stavrides says that heterotopias should be considered "not as places of otherness but as passages towards otherness" (*ibid.*). In a footnote, quoting his own article on heterotopias and urban space, he says that heterotopias "mark an osmosis between situated identities" (*ibid.*; Stavrides 2007: 178) and thus become important for social transformation. This is another sign of the relevance of the in-between, the gathering threshold, and the trans-dividual assemblage. Stavrides also remarks that heterotopias "as passages are moving places, places from which whatever is happening has departed from the previous order without a given destination" (2019: 152–154). Foucault himself speaks of a heterotopia as a mirror – a different mirror, to be sure, from the one of utopia, the "placeless place" (Foucault 1998: 179). He says, "Due to the mirror, I discover myself absent at the place where I am, since I see myself over there" (*ibid.*). He continues, "The mirror functions as a heterotopia in the sense that it makes this place I occupy at the moment I look at myself in the glass both utterly real . . . and utterly unreal" (*ibid.*). The generic and accidental glass, more of a threshold than a mirror glass, a window pane for instance, which includes the function of a mirror to an extent, but it is not properly a mirror, has an even stronger heterotopic potential, for it may dislocate and disrupt (disturb) reality and the perception of reality even more. It is a phenomenon of refraction, or even diffraction if there is a crack, an open wound, rather than reflection. The place projected by and through the glass is still "utterly real . . . and utterly unreal," but because it is not simply a vision that returns to the place of the viewer but extends into a new place of immanence, with new figures and contours – perhaps imaginary, or transfigured (disfigured) lines and forms – it creates difference as difference, namely a precarious, contingent, and accidental difference. Yet, because of a moment (and a movement) of ontological convergence (the convergence of contingency and necessity), the accidental here takes on the quality of the essential by storming and disintegrating it.

It is this type of difference (precarious, contingent, and accidental), this heterotopia, which, as Catherine Malabou says at the very end of *Ontology of the Accident* (2012), "dangerously disfigure[s] the meaning of essence" (91). The meaning of essence here also means the metaphysics of subjectivity. The subject is disfigured, and its place transfigured, becoming another place, the place of otherness. Malabou speaks of "the power of plasticity" (1), which has an "ontological and existential explosive" importance for "subjectivity and identity" (5). There is here a "damned" (3) passage, or threshold, whereby a person can be completely transformed. Malabou says, "As a result of serious trauma, or sometimes for no reason at all, the path splits and a new, unprecedented persona comes to live with the former person, and eventually takes up all the room" (1). She speaks of "transformations that are attacks on the individual" (2), an "explosive plasticity," which might place us "outside of time" (3). Malabou also calls this phenomenon "pathological plasticity, a plasticity that does not repair" (6). It amounts to "the deserting of subjectivity" (*ibid.*). It is "the distancing of the individual who becomes a stranger to herself, who no longer recognizes anyone, who no longer recognizes herself, who no longer remembers her self" (*ibid.*). Malabou's somewhat uneven book has a brutal and scary start – yet quite real, tempered by a literary and philosophical elaboration on the theme of transformation. What is important for us, from the viewpoint of a philosophy of thresholds, is the problem of capture and flight, namely, how when flight becomes impossible (because of a trauma or for no apparent reason at all), the only thing left to do is fleeing "the impossibility of fleeing itself" (11) by abandoning one's identity and becoming "a *form* of flight" (*ibid.*), that is to say, an *essential/accidental difference*, an entirely different being.

Malabou says that "in classic metamorphoses, transformation intervenes in place of flight" (10). But, she continues, "metamorphoses by destruction is not the same as flight; it is rather the form of the impossibility of fleeing" (*ibid.*). This is a paradoxical situation, one of total capture in which, however, a threshold appears that is not a threshold, but a return to an impossible self, an impossible identity. This happens in situations in which "a pain or malaise push a person towards an outside that does not exist" (*ibid.*). It is, Malabou says, the "impossibility of flight where flight presents the only possible solution" (*ibid.*).

Destructive plasticity is then "the formation of a *form* of flight" (11). The emphasis on the word 'form' is very important because it indicates the formation of an absolutely and radically new identity, a paradoxically new being. It is "the appearance or formation of alterity where the other is lacking" (*ibid.*), a frightening situation. It is a disfigured and distorted return to the self as an other, and to an absent self. No flight or escape left, the "only other that exists in this circumstance is being other to the self" (*ibid.*). It is a double capture, a double exception, in which the threshold returns to itself as the absence of a threshold. Although Malabou says that this transformation is still a form of salvation, "a strange salvation" (12), though, it is also true that the alterity thus formed does not belong in the heterotopic domain, but in the dystopic one, "an alterity that the pursuer cannot assimilate" (*ibid.*). Not being able to flee makes people become "strangers to themselves" (13), "new people, others, re-engendered, belonging to a different species" (*ibid.*). With a reference to Deleuze and Guattari, Malabou speaks of a replacement of subjectivity (16). But the most important point is that for Malabou, differently than for Deleuze and Guattari, whose reading of Kafka she is here considering, the passage from one form to the other is not one in which "form can be thought separately from the nature of the being that transforms itself" (17). This is indeed the precise meaning of the title of her book, *Ontology of the Accident*. The accident as such acquires full ontological status. Malabou says that for Deleuze and Guattari "a form . . . can do nothing but freeze becoming" (*ibid.*). However, for Malabou this has to do with the inability of the critique of metaphysics to denounce the constant metaphysical "dissociation of essence and form" (*ibid.*). It seems that for Malabou, Deleuze and Guattari's – as well as others' – privileging the constant process of (a formless) becoming – "becoming-animal" rather than "becoming *an* animal" – as well as the constant individuating process, rather than individuation as such, ultimately completely does away with the concept of form, which "is absurd" (*ibid.*). It is as if, she says colorfully, "in the evening, form could be left hanging like a garment on the chair of being or essence" (*ibid.*). This is an important point, but it is problematic, too. Obviously, to say that there is no underlying formlessness upon which transformations and metamorphoses take place makes a lot of sense from the viewpoint of the critique of metaphysics. Yet, to indicate that one should focus on the (sudden) actualization of different forms, rather than on the transformative process itself, seems to suggest that new forms emerge out of nothing, or nowhere, and they are simply occurrences, folds, *accidents*, exhausting all potency of being in their actualization. To be sure, discrete occurrences, folds, and accidents constitute an important part of reality, the contingent and unpredictable, which "without hope of return, dangerously disfigure the meaning of essence" (91). And they do, in fact, change things forever. Yet, the potency that fuels and sustains their (at times terrifying) actualization, that is, the transformative process itself, does not end with them, it is not exhausted thereby. Malabou is correct in denouncing the fact that in metaphysics, "form can always change, but the nature of being persists" (17). This is a problem. But if it is not "the nature of being" that persists, it is perhaps, just like with Heraclitus, change itself. So perhaps the ontological meaning of the accident does not reside in the form as such, in any given form, but in the trans-forming process itself.

With the notion of plasticity, Malabou intends to "find a way to think about a mutation that engages both form and being, a new form that is literally a form of being" (*ibid.*). 'A form of being' means something entirely different from 'a form of appearance,' typical of the tradition of metaphysics. Indeed, as we know from Heidegger (or from Anaxagoras, for that matter), there is always something that does not appear in the appearance. Contrary to this, 'a form of being' would be its own essence, a haecceitas, a thisness, a singularity, which has no reserve of becoming, but is entirely the contingency and accident that it is. While this seems to bridge the metaphysical split between being and becoming, to "impose upon becoming the character of being," as Nietzsche says (1968: #617), it yields a conception of a scattered reality, where every event, every accident, has its own absolute boundaries, its sudden – not appearance – but full existence (full of essence). Yet, perhaps underemphasized (or totally overlooked) would be the notion and reality of the threshold – unless, that is, the threshold, the door, is the accident itself. But here, too, in the abrupt passage from one state to the other, from one identity to the other, what seem to be at risk of losing significance are the metastable, transdividual passage and the resulting assemblage(s) where individual identity vanishes. Perhaps it is not the case that one goes from one identity to another, but rather that one experiences the absence of identity that has always already been there. The impossibility of fleeing is a form of absolute capture, a situation without thresholds, as "the formation of a *form* of flight" (Malabou 2012: 11). With no exit, it is a bouncing back into a nonexistent or absent self. Malabou speaks of "the fabrication of a new persona, a novel form of life, without anything in common with a preceding form" (18). This seems problematic. Perhaps there remains a too strong focus on identity and individuality; less on the trans-dividual and singular, the common and plural, the tensions and struggles. What is important here is that there is "absence from the self" (19), a "void of subjectivity" (24), a "distancing of the individual who becomes an ontological refugee" (*ibid.*). This in-dividual "is not the other *of* someone" (*ibid.*), but a mere other, an other with no self and no subjectivity, open to either the capture of number or the flight of singularity. This plastic other, which is what we most essentially are, is the accident as such, in its innermost essence and in its outward form; it is the threshold, border, or door. There is no other behind this other, and there is no self to return to: no principle, no *arkhē*. The place of an absence, the absence of a place: the changeable and transformable take the place of 'normal identity' (31); plasticity, "the possibility of being transformed without being destroyed" (44), replaces fixed identity, individuality, and subjectivity.

In *Signs and Machines* (2014), Maurizio Lazzarato addresses Guattari's existential (non-discursive) dimension of the production of subjectivity, of transitional subjectivities (208), to be precise, and singularities. Although the term subjectivity is used by both Lazzarato and Guattari, it is clear that what takes place in "existentialization" (207), in the "transversality of subjectivity" (208), is beyond the metaphysics of the subject and subjectivity on account of its dynamic process of individuation, its production. In the production of subjectivity, subjectivity itself is obviously not a pre-constituted and fixed essence, but the temporary (hence, never fully completed) result of an unfolding process. Malabou's notion of plasticity we have seen above very well renders the meaning of this process. The new form is not the form of appearance of something else, an accidental modification of the essence, but it is an essential difference, a true transformation, a new ontological formation. But subjectivity as such, in its modality of either subjection or subjectivation, possibly resists this transformation and remains in the same situation of capture: it remains *in the same*, unable to truly become an other. The question one might pose for Malabou is the question of *what* exactly is transformed without being destroyed. Perhaps the answer is that this 'what' is precisely the place (or mechanism) of an absence, a "void of subjectivity," as we have seen (Malabou 2012: 24); in other words, the 'what' is not there. It is in this sense that the concept of singularity (always constituted by a multiplicity, a plurality, and constantly individuating) is superior to that of subjectivity. The opposite of singularity is *number*, any number and many numbers, namely, seriality. Number, or seriality, is the negation of transversality and transitionality, of singularity and trans-dividuality. If what is transversal and transitional is a subjectivity, many subjectivities, the result is probably intersubjectivity rather than a becoming-threshold, a gathering, and a trans-dividual assemblage, which has abandoned any regard, any nostalgia, for the 'what' and the 'who' of origin, and has become a mode, a 'how' of expression. This is true not only for any given person, but even more so for collectivities, social movements and struggles – given especially the heterogeneity of struggles, as Mezzadra and Neilson (2019) say, where plasticity and fluidity are very important. Hence, it is also true of historical change, modes of production and consumption, as Marx already showed in the introduction to the *Grundrisse* speaking precisely of "essential difference" in this respect (Marx 1973: 85).

Singularities multiply and proliferate. In one of Guattari's seminars considered by Lazzarato in *Signs and Machines*, "Singularité et complexité," the process of singularization is seen as "proliferating singularities" (Guattari 1985: 10). For Guattari, a singularity is never found by itself ("on n'a jamais de singularité en soi" – *ibid.*). Proliferating singularities are "transpersonal, postpersonal, beyond the person" (*ibid.*). They engage "orders, institutions, movements" (*ibid.*). Guattari addresses the main problem we have with subjectivity when, at the outset of his seminar, he says that "subjectivity has become ... an object of mass production, just another commodity" and that we should think about "other modes of subjectivation" (1). These other modes are what I prefer to call singularities, without any further regard for subjectivity. The question is conceptual, not at all terminological. Singularity makes it easier to think the existential fluidity and plasticity demanded by a political ontology of thresholds, of networks and assemblages. It is close to the concept Leibniz highlights in speaking of the notion of an individual substance, thisness, or monad. Yet, differently from Leibniz's monads, Guattari says that these *existential singularities* are "singular monads, finite monads, which pose the question of the existential boundary," thus the question of their singular finitude (12). They are existential objects, transitional subjectivities, as well as "points of auto-existentialization . . . that cross thresholds" (Guattari 1985: 12). Guattari says, "The singular trait develops its world" (11). Yet, singularity is neither an individual nor a collective subjectivity, but precisely a threshold and, within finitude, a tension beyond finitude. In Chapter Eight, we will see how Paolo Virno (2004) defines the individuated singularity, the subject, as "a battlefield" (78). For now, it is important to keep in mind the meaning of the threshold beyond the limit; in other words, what always defies complete individuation, and thus, potentially, capture. The singular developing its world as a finite yet open monad, though individuated at any given moment, becomes a threshold, constantly infinitizing itself, and constantly returning to the finite. But it is through the process of singularization, not subjectivation, that whatever-is-not-one reaches into the common.

As we conclude this chapter, a word should be said about the dynamics of struggle in the tension between capture and escape, that is to say, the threshold and line of flight. This also goes back to the issues of violence, counterviolence and antiviolence (civility), as well as, in particular, to the form of violence that Walter Benjamin calls "divine." But the point precisely is that it is *struggle* rather than unqualified violence that is the focus here. In *The Politics of Operations*, Mezzadra and Neilson ask the question, "What is a struggle?" (2019: 186). After reviewing various ways in which this question can be (and has been) answered, they say that their understanding of struggle is close to "what Chantal Mouffe (2005, 20) calls 'antagonism,' which describes a situation in which adversaries have no common ground" (187). Essentially, however, they highlight the important dimension of the contingency of struggle, namely, "the moment of political productivity and creativity inherent to struggle" (*ibid.*). Moving away from both the Clausewitzian model of struggle as opposition of forces, "a relation of enmity," and the Hegelian and Marxian (Western Marxism's) emphasis on consciousness, they approach struggle "through the question of political subjectivity and its production" (*ibid.*) in a way that the heterogeneity of struggle corresponds to that of "the uneven and changing space and time of contemporary capitalism" (188). Yet, it is not at all a reaction to the logic of contemporary capitalism. Mezzadra and Neilson call attention to the way in which "struggle is driven by a production of subjectivity that is something more than a reaction to the contradictions and operations of capital or a practice of resistance that is determined by the forces that oppose it" (*ibid.*). In line with the tradition of the Italian Autonomist movement, thinkers such as Mario Tronti and Antonio Negri, among others, but also with the thought of Michel Foucault, they "take struggles in the field of subjectivation as a key reference to reframe the very notions and manifestations of domination and exploitation" (189). As they move to the question of "boundary struggles" (192), the concepts of threshold and singularization come to mind. Essentially, what they call subjectivation is singularization, that is, the singular expressing the common – a line of flight from capture, certainly not the obverse form of subjection. It is, as I have often metaphorically put it, the gathering at the threshold, but also becoming-thresholds and singularly building, doing, and *making* the common within them. As Mezzadra and Neilson say, "the making of the common is not necessarily a debordering project but one that can involve the institution and management of borders in ways that do not heed the social relation of capital" (196). In this, they include "the kind of territorial borders implied by Indigenous sovereignty claims" (*ibid.*). If it is not a debordering project, it still is an exit from the paradigm of number, finding and occupying the threshold beyond the limit, the boundary, expressing the common in and through the singular, the multiplicity of singularities.

3

Subversions

SEVEN
A Passage to Art

The discourse on art and labor has greatly changed recently, and any attempt to distinguish between artistic and 'mere' production stumbles upon the demands and difficulties of the neoliberal digital, sharing and gig economy.[1] Rather interestingly, the word 'gig' originates in the art world, particularly music. As Morgan and Nelligan say, "More workers are now living like musicians – working precariously from gig to gig" (2018: Loc 229). This, however, does not mean that all production is now geared toward the creation of artworks in the traditional sense – the sense illustrated by Heidegger (1971) in *The Origin of the Work of Art*, for instance. Rather, what this means is that living and working in the entrepreneurial and debt society entails a constant effort at producing one's own subsistence, one's own means of production even, as well as one's own self: one's subjectivity, or singularity.

The distance between art and labor has shrunk, or disappeared, in the same way in which the distance between life and work has been taken away by all those activities whose produced value is immeasurable and that virtually entail a 24/7 working lifestyle. This is particularly evident in all uberized forms of labor, in the field of care, the IT jobs, the arts proper, but also in the nightmarish and often tragic work of migrants as they cross continents and oceans fleeing wars and economic devastation in search of a better future.[2] This is work that never ends, producing value that cannot be measured and entailing a constant renewal and sharpening of creative skills as well as a permanent intersectional expenditure of physical, mental, and emotional forces.

The situation is one in which subjectivities (and really, singularities) are produced in conditions of often great subjection. At times, this subjection is confirmed in and by the new subjectivities produced. This is the case when a sense of conformity is internalized to the point that subjection is, as it were, 'voluntarily' accepted and servitude 'voluntarily' entered into. Other times – and our hope is that this might increasingly be the most common occurrence – the new subjectivities are produced on the basis of a more or less clear, conscious, and planned project of liberation; they are thus, properly speaking, singularities. This happens when a subversion of understood conditions of subjection is attempted and initiated. What follows in this case is a transformation, a transfiguration, of what is originally taken as the self – the making of entirely new singularities, perhaps equal, in a Nietzschean manner, to artworks. In the first instance, when subjection and servitude are internalized and confirmed, we have the production of discreet individuals under the illusion of independence and freedom. In the second instance, the transfiguration happens *in* the common and is *of* the common. In both instances, there is a process of transindividuation at work.[3] The difference lies in accepting or refusing to accept the dictates of discipline and control imposed by capital, biopower, and the politics of number. In other words, the difference lies in obedience or refusal and resistance (and rebellion). Again, in the first instance, the fictional notion of the free and independent individual, the "*sovereign individual* . . . master of a *free* will" (Nietzsche 1967: 59), "a kingdom within a kingdom" (Spinoza 1992: 102; cf. Read 2016) appears as real to a degree. In the second instance, this notion is shattered, or simply evaded, by engaging in a process of trans-dividuation and true liberation. This process entails an understanding of being-with, the ontological constitution of a plural singularity, and the common.[4] Indeed, in this second instance, the ontological, constitutive process is more one of trans-dividuation than transindividuation.

At times, the word subjectivity, or even singularity, is used as a magic word, as if it by default indicated a progressive or even revolutionary mentality and existence. In truth, even subjected subjectivities are, precisely, subjectivities. Furthermore, we are all subjected, to various degrees. Subjectivity, or singularity, is, as I have noted above, always the temporary result of a process of transindividuation or trans-dividuation. But transindividuation can take different directions, and the point, as Jason Read notes in his book on transindividuality (Read 2016), is not to simply say that everything is transindividual; rather, the point is to understand why and how the process of transindividuation often disappears from the result and what appears instead is the unity of the free and independent individual, masking the process itself. Indeed, the central historical question in Read's book is, "How can social relations produce their own effacement?" (5). He says that transindividuality, or transindividuation, can be examined from an ontological and historical viewpoint. In particular, he says that "while the ontological question is to understand how it is that the individual emerges from collective conditions, the historical question is how to grasp the effacement of the collective conditions of individuation" (*ibid.*). In this book, I am also considering the notion of trans-dividuation and whether this might not be a better way of explaining the making of true, non-subjected, and free singularities.

This does not mean that one chooses between servitude and liberation, subjection and freedom in a voluntaristic way, which is the way criticized by Read, following in particular the thought of Spinoza and Marx. Other authors also take the same position in relation to the question of free choice. Notably, Frédéric Lordon, in his book on capitalism and desire, strongly rejects the notion that there is such a situation in which one freely chooses. His ideas are also, like in the case of Read, particularly shaped by the thought of Spinoza (and that of Marx). Indeed, he says, that there is no voluntary servitude, but only (and always) passionate servitude. The difference between servitude and freedom lies in understanding the causes of our passions (in keeping with Spinoza), but also, and consequently, in a movement of rupture, in the power to act. Lordon says, "When the indignation that gets people moving prevails over the *obsequium* that makes them stay put, a new affective vector is formed, and individuals who used to be determined to respect institutional norms (for example, those of the employment relation) are suddenly determined to sedition" (2014: 140). Although the word 'individuals' is used here, it is obvious that we are on the plane of transindividuality, which includes the preindividual play of affective forces as well. Indeed, Lordon emphasizes that it is not a matter of using one's free will, but of following one's sensuous and emotional disposition and inclination. He says that indignation "overturns the affective equilibria that have until then determined the subjects to submit to institutional relations, and leads them to desire to live, not according to their free will, but *as it pleases them – ex suo ingenio –* which implies, not some miraculous leap into the unconditioned, but a step into a life *determined in another way*" (141; emphasis in the original). Obviously, one way in which this happens is through the refusal of work, which is really ultimately also a refusal to be forced to be *one*. As Stevphen Shukaitis says in the chapter called "Learning Not to Labor" in his recent book, "The refusal of work plays a key role in fermenting class struggle as it provides a framework for moving from discontent to action, underpinned by a concrete utopian desire to reduce and, if possible, eliminate the influence of work over social life" (2016: 89). Work is here obviously understood, as it should be, as a form of servitude and capture. "Learning Not to Labor," in Shukaitis' book refers to the important title by Paul Willis, *Learning to Labor* (1977) – important even for the discourse on art and labor we are drawing here. The difference is that the mechanism of social reproduction analyzed and described by Willis, which leads working class kids to work in the factory, has been altered in many ways, as precarity and disposability have become increasingly more predominant. For Shukaitis the question is then how to develop a kind of "zerowork training" (88) able to produce new forms of subjectivation, where "the *refusal* of work" is also "the *refusing* of the social energies of such refusal back into supporting the continued affective existence and capacities of other forms of life and ways of being together" (98). This is, I believe, what the return of labor to itself, and the passage to art, also means.

Perhaps this is what the production of rebellious subjectivities, that is, singularities, implies: a rupture driven by desire toward *another way* that is both affective and artistic. In addition to its Spinozian character, this rupture is also in line with the philosophies of Nietzsche and Marx. It is the new direction pointed out by Nietzsche when, after the abolition of metaphysics, after the destructive moment, he also sees in art and the sensuous a constructive going beyond, an immanent transcendence. Thus, he says, "An anti-metaphysical view of the world – yes, but an artistic one" (1968: #1048). He also says that art is to become "the real task of life" (#853, IV). This does not mean that people have necessarily to engage with one of the fine arts; rather, it means that life itself should be produced artistically. In fact, he continues, "art as life's *metaphysical* activity" (*ibid.*). This is obviously no longer the metaphysics of the Platonic tradition, which Nietzsche wants to destroy. It is not the metaphysics of the split between a real world of ideas and a world of mere appearances. In fact, both worlds are destroyed. In *The Twilight of the Idols*, Nietzsche says, "The 'real' world – an idea no longer of any use, not even a duty any longer – an idea grown useless, superfluous, *consequently* a refuted idea: let us abolish it!" Yet, with the abolition of the 'real' world, the world of appearances is also abolished. Nietzsche continues, "We have abolished the real world. What world is left? the apparent world perhaps? . . . But no! *with the real world we have abolished the apparent world!*" (Nietzsche 1990: 50–51). What remains is *this world, the world we are*.[5] It is in this sense that one understands the 'metaphysical,' *ontological*, role of art. It is part of a poetic metaphysics, a poetic ontology, in Vico's sense of the word. Indeed, for Vico (1968), the true is the same as the made, and *poiesis* and *praxis* are together responsible for the constitution of the self, the common, and the world – in a word, of singularities. It is interesting that, in this way, Vico's poetic doing and making and Nietzsche's aesthetic overcoming of metaphysics announce a world in which the production of what one is (and constantly is not), the production of singularities, has indeed become *the real task of life* – real, but ultimately also necessary and, often in a negative sense (such as when it is looked at through the logic of debt), a serious and inescapable injunction.[6]

As for Marx, we can look at the question of the emancipation of the senses in the *Economic and Philosophical Manuscripts of 1844*. In line with the emphasis on subjectivity present in the *Theses on Feuerbach*, here Marx speaks of the changes – a rupture – in the human subject following the coming of a communist future, the abolition of private property. He says, "The supersession of private property is therefore the complete *emancipa-

tion of all human senses and attributes, but it is this emancipation precisely because these senses and attributes have become *human*, subjectively as well as objectively" (1975: 352). Here, too, there is a poetic and practical ontology. Marx says, "The *senses* have therefore become *theoreticians* in their immediate praxis" (*ibid.*). He also says, "The eye has become a *human* eye, just as its *object* has become a social, *human* object" (*ibid.*). Just as in Nietzsche the sensuous is what remains after the destruction of metaphysics, and, following the senses with their "subtlety, plenitude, and power" (Nietzsche 1968: #617), the world becomes art, a work of art, or work as art, so in Marx the senses go back to *their immediate praxis*. The result is a transformation, or transfiguration, of the world and of the subject – a making of new subjectivities, or singularities.

Yet, the ideas of the emancipation of the senses and of art as the real task of life have to be seen in relation to the new technologies that call into question the notion of the simply human; that is to say, they have to be considered in the context of the machinic assemblage, of the trans-dividual relation of humans and machines (of which more will be said later), and of the common. Indeed, it is not the case – and certainly that was not the case with Marx – that an individual as such could overcome the rift between necessity and contingency, theory and praxis, desire and action. To be sure, the 'individual' is always social – a trans-dividuation, though that may often not appear to be the case. Indeed, the lingering of appearance (of *this* appearance) may in itself be the problem: appearance and representation. Indeed, the emancipation of the senses and the notion of art as the real task of life imply a critique of appearance and representation – and, for that matter, of sovereignty. Yet, we still have to start from the fundamental idea that representation is the exact opposite of care; *sovereignty* is the exact opposite of care. Yet, care is a form of power: power-to instead of power-over, this latter describing sovereignty and representation. From here we can proceed to an appreciation of what the rupture we have been describing might entail in progressive and revolutionary ways.

Art is always a form of labor, in the generic sense of making and doing. Indeed, as I wrote in *Labor of Fire*, "how can art be something other than labor?" (Gullì 2005: 185). Labor is not always art, but in the neoliberal economy the distinction between the two categories is, as we have seen, complicated by the fact that work is not simply an activity geared toward the production of external commodities, of value congealed in those commodities, and the surplus-value that follows from that, but it entails a production of the self, of the subjectivity of the worker, and in this sense it also entails the implementation of creative skills that one might usually associate with artistic production. They also produce a surplus. Art can no longer claim to be an independent and separate realm. Indeed, there is perhaps no art as such anymore. I say this in the sense meant by Marx as he discusses abstract labor, *"labour pure and simple,*" in the *Grundrisse* (1973: 296). There he says that "labour loses all the characteristics of art; as its particular skill becomes something more and more abstract and irrelevant, and as it becomes more and more a *purely abstract activity*" (297; emphasis in the original).[7] In the age of finance capital, this is even more important than at Marx's time. Certainly, Marx's idea of labor "as *absolute poverty*" on the one hand and as "the *general possibility* of wealth" on the other, a split between the objective and subjective dispositions of labor (296), is even more apparent today than in the second half of the nineteenth century. Marx says that labor is *absolute poverty* "not as shortage, but as total exclusion of objective wealth," (*ibid.*), while it is "the *general possibility* of wealth as subject and as activity" (*ibid.*). The figure of the indebted man described by Maurizio Lazzarato (2012), with the constant injunction to become an entrepreneur of the self, is a perfect illustration of this apparent contradiction, or rather of the contradiction that follows "from the essence of labour, such as it is *presupposed* by capital as its contradiction and as its contradictory being, and such as it, in turn, presupposes capital" (Marx 1973: 296).

In 1967, Guy Debord wrote, "Art's declaration of independence is thus the beginning of the end of art" (1995: 133). The end of art, we now see, means its diffusion throughout society, "in the social factory" (Hardt and Negri 2017: 175–178), through "social production" (173). As Hardt and Negri say, "Value is produced in the social factory that stretches across the entire social terrain and throughout the sites of production and reproduction" (175). This diffusion, in turn, means that all laboring activities, all life activities, have to have elements and dimensions that perhaps in the past belonged to art proper. So, if on the one hand, as Marx says, labor, as abstract labor "loses all the characteristics of art" (1973: 296) – and this is the case under the industrial regime of production – it needs, on the other hand, to become *artful* in the new economy of debt and finance, "an apparatus that directly captures and extracts value from social production" (Hardt and Negri 2017: 171). For an increasing number of people, making a living, even at the level of mere survival, implies the ability to joggle many temporary jobs all at the same time, to move from place to place, within the same ("creative") city or across countries and continents – with the important psychological and existential toll that all this takes. This is the meaning of the gig economy. In a very recent book by George Morgan and Pariece Nelligan (2018), the notion of the positive importance of creativity in the neoliberal economy is rightly called into question. With a reference, in particular, to Richard Florida's popular book, *The Rise of the Creative Class* (2003), Morgan and Nelligan point out an interesting passage from *knowledge* to *creativity* as a "key buzzword for regeneration" (Loc 140) within the narrative of capital at the end of the twentieth and the beginning of the twenty-first centuries. They also say that this is "true not only in the West but also in developing economies, where creativity is seen as a key to fast-track modernization, as well as in China, where creativity is seen as a necessary step in the passage from a low-labour cost-manufacturing centre to a new economy" (Loc 145–150). As their title clearly says, the truth of the matter is that we are in the midst of a creativity hoax. First of all, as they point out, there is no longer a distinction between creative and non-creative occupations. This really means that creativity becomes a necessity. Morgan and Nelligan say, "To survive, to maintain some semblance of continuity in working life in the face of underemployment or unemployment, often means that workers have to learn how to sell their skills in volatile marketplaces, to become entrepreneurial" (Loc 214). They call this figure of labor *"labile labour*: mobile, spontaneous, malleable and capable of being aroused by new vocational possibilities" (Loc 1728). We have already seen this in relation to the debt society, with a reference to Lazzarato's book, and we will say more about it later by looking at an interesting take by Hardt and Negri on the figure of the entrepreneur. What is important now is to note Morgan and Nelligan's central argument, which is that "the idea of creative economy is in part a discursive trick concerned with promoting flexibility and mobility of labour. It deflects ambition and encourages workers to see their skills as transferable and abstract rather than particular and grounded" (Loc 219). Indeed, "Capitalism's co-option of the idea of creativity is one of the more spectacular discursive operations of recent history" (Loc 512). They also say that this co-option "conceals the bohemian tradition that associates art with resistance to capitalism" (*ibid.*). It is no longer simply a matter of removing from labor all the characteristics of art. In the age of finance and the gig economy, the extraction of value, as Hardt and Negri point out, also implies financial capital's own "abstraction from production and its capacity to rule at a distance" (2017: 163). They explain, "The key to finance – and capitalist accumulation as a whole – is how value is extracted from wealth that resides elsewhere, both the wealth of the earth and the wealth that results from social cooperation and interaction. This is the link between abstraction and extraction" (164). The illusion of a diffused creativity is indeed very often the mask for a conformity brought about by a subtle discipline and methods of control whose aim is the production of what Michel Foucault called *docile bodies*, obedient and useful at the same time – indeed, useful because obedient (Foucault 1977). This, however, does not eliminate the possibility of creativity as rupture and as a singular power for radical change.

The issue of precarity is also taken up by Gregory Sholette in *Dark Matter* (2010). Sholette also speaks of the *social factory* and "the politics of invisibility" (5), which obviously create an illusory dimension of freedom and creativity. Very pointedly, he says that "enterprise culture requires a kind of enforced creativity that is imposed on all forms of labor" (7). Moreover, as Stevphen Shukaitis says, "The arts world becomes a laboratory where the post-Fordist ethic is developed and then generalized beyond it" (2016: 94). This is a very important point because it helps us bridge the discursive gap between art and labor. To repeat a thought we have already considered above, but put very well by Sholette, "Workers, whose livelihoods have been made increasingly precarious by the collapse of the traditional social welfare state, are expected to be forever ready to retrain themselves at their own expense (or their own debt), to labor continuously even when at home or on vacation, and finally, they are expected to be constantly creative, to think like an artist" (2010: 7). The debt and gig economy again! A society in which what is common is really the paradoxical figure of a creativity that has become pure abstraction and a conformity that leads into a deformity of the soul. Sholette acknowledges the new link between creativity and value, which is the same as what Hardt and Negri address as the abstraction/extraction nexus in the age of finance, the capture and extraction of value from social production (2017: 170–171). In this sense, the deformity of souls is also a deformity of bodies, just as Marx also says in an amazing passage of the *Economic and Philosophical Manuscripts*: "It is true that labour produces marvels for the rich, but it produces privation for the worker. It produces palaces, but hovels for the worker. It produces beauty, but deformity for the worker. It replaces labour by machines, but it casts some of the workers back into barbarous forms of labour and turns others into machines. It produces intelligence, but it produces idiocy and cretinism for the worker" (Marx 1975: 325–326). Indeed, he also writes, "the more his product is shaped, the more misshapen the worker" (325). Yet, it is precisely this removal into the realm of abstraction, this forced invisibility, which, even in a distorted way, makes things visible again. This new visibility depends on the "sheer abundance and precariousness" of "this apparent surplus army" of labor and art (Sholette 2010: 16) – this *labile labor* for Morgan and Nelligan, as we have seen. Sholette says, "Young artists, often working collectively, have begun to address their relationship to work" (*ibid.*), demanding a wage, in a move similar to the wages for housework movement, in what Sholette calls an *"other* productivity" (19).[8]

For Debord, art's decay indicates that "a new common language has yet to be found" (1995: 133). This "new common language," which is *praxis* and *poiesis* at the same time, is now found at the level of everyday life, in the context of life that has become work, of work that has become life. The question of a common language, or simply of the common, has to do with representation, sovereignty, and care. I have already noted how representation and care are opposites, but this relationship of opposition also applies to sovereignty and care.[9] Indeed, representation and sovereignty are very closely related. All sovereignty includes representation, and all representation certainly has moments of sovereignty. The new common language sought by Debord takes the form of constituent power in the sense in which Hardt and Negri reconceptualize it in *Assem-*

bly, as "a widespread and multitudinous germination of the desire for freedom and equality" (2017: 35). They speak of decision-making powers outside the paradigm of sovereignty and representation, as a way of transforming society according to "a right to the common" (*ibid.*). They call this constituent power "a composition of diverse constituent singularities" (36) and stress the fact that it is "no longer compatible with representation and sovereignty" (37). This critique of sovereignty and representation is very important because even today we are far from having effectively taken distance from it, at the institutional level as well as (sadly) often in social movements. It is true that, as Hardt and Negri say, "the democratic claims of political representation are becoming ever more widely recognized as hollow and, similarly, speaking in the name of others is becoming proscribed in social movements" (*ibid.*). This is certainly an important and visible tendency. Yet, the destruction of old forms of power and domination, based on sovereignty and representation, what they later call a "destituent project" (223), is of course still under way – far from having been accomplished, and those entrenched institutional and cultural claims to representing others and deciding about the desire and freedom of others are still very strong. An instance of this is the sense of entitlement inherent in the structures of patriarchy and whiteness, as is well known.[10] Hardt and Negri's important notion of the invention of nonsovereign institutions (37–39), which is part of the constituent project (223), constitutes the site of current and future struggles for a powerful political ontology, which is poetic and practical at the same time: a transfiguration, a reconfiguration, or a transformation and reconstitution of social existence as a whole. Obviously, this project rules out a nostalgic return to the past, which would be precisely a move backward rather than forward. Hardt and Negri are also very adamant about this extremely important point, often misunderstood by those who pose as leaders in social movements. They say, "Recognizing, however, that the violent and bloody construction of private property throughout the world involved the suppression of social forms of sharing wealth – land, most importantly – should not lead us to conceive the common in terms of precapitalist social forms or to yearn for their re-creation" (97–98). As I have noted, this is sadly often not understood, and, especially in those experiences of a return to the land and to (a romanticized conception of) nature, there is at times a tendency, at the theoretical as well as practical level, toward such a re-creation. Yet, Hardt and Negri point out, "In many cases the precapitalist forms of community and systems for sharing wealth were characterized by disgusting, patriarchal, hierarchical modes of division and control" (98). And they conclude, "Instead of gazing back prior to capitalist private property we need to look beyond it" (*ibid.*). This is also the meaning of a new common language outside of the paradigm of sovereignty and representation – a language of immediacy, of the emancipation of the senses, and of true aesthetic (*transvaluated*) value. This is of course the positive way in which art and labor, creativity and habit, can cooperate again – perhaps breaking their confinement in abstraction and value. Obviously, these nonsovereign institutions must be true artworks, not a mere formal rearrangement of the same: they are really trans-stitutions. As Hardt and Negri say, this new constituent power "must be mixed with social behaviors and new technologies of subsistence, resistance, and transformation of life" (41). More than just a political reality, it goes to the bottom of social, everyday life, to the material and singular conditions of existence – without becoming a matter of identity.

But what is art proper? For Heidegger, we need to distinguish between creating and making: creating has its end in itself; making has an end other than itself. Both belong to *poiesis*, to production as 'bringing forth.' In *The Origin of the Work of Art*, Heidegger distinguishes between creating and mere making (Heidegger 1971). He says, "We think of creation as a bringing forth. But the making of equipment, too, is a bringing forth. Handicraft . . . does not, to be sure, create works, not even when we contrast, as we must, the handmade with the factory product" (58). Then he asks, "But what is it that distinguishes bringing forth as creation from bringing forth in the mode of making?" (*ibid*.). What distinguishes them, for Heidegger, is poetry: "The Nature [*Wesen*] of art is poetry. The nature [*Wesen*] of poetry is the funding of truth" (75).[11] Perhaps today there is no longer creation in the sense understood by Heidegger and all bringing forth happens in the mode of making – and a *machinic*, algorithmic, making at that. Perhaps part of the problem is that, as Hardt and Negri point out, Heidegger's viewpoint is "preindustrial and even precapitalist" (2017: 109). Yet, the notion of creativity cannot be left to neo-liberal ideology, "the eureka myth" of Silicon Valley (Morgan and Nelligan 2018: Loc 492), and the injunction to become one's own entrepreneur under penalty of debt and death. As Hardt and Negri say, living labor exceeds this biopolitical framing. They say that "as it becomes an increasingly social power, living labor (and life activity more generally) operates as an ever more independent activity, outside the structures of discipline that capital commands" (2017: 116). This is what is ultimately responsible for the production of new subjectivities, singularities of rupture. In *Labor of Fire* (2005), the argument was that creative labor is the form of living labor which is *not* productive (in the sense of capital), namely, neither-productive-nor-unproductive. The concept of creativity has certainly been co-opted by neoliberalism today, yet that does not mean that its potency – the potency of living and creative labor – has ceased to exist as a mode of disruption and transformation. To the contrary, it has reached an inner depth, the level of a subterranean fire, where labor returns to itself, and art also returns to itself – a return which is equally a revolving and spinning. This is what is usually known as the production of subjectivities, or singularities, which is perhaps the most important aspect of the relationship between art and labor today. This is also what, as we have seen, eminently happens at the border, at any border.

Speaking of the social factory, Morgan and Nelligan say that consumers "are also, in a sense, producers (e.g., as in online gaming) and that labour happens away from the factory floor in the traditional sense" (2018: Loc 505). They say that a new category of workers, with special, 'creative,' skills and habits "play a central role in the production chain because symbolic and knowledge inputs contribute much more to a commodity's value than does the labour of those on the assembly lines" (*ibid.*). Obviously, as virtually all those who write on these issues also do, Morgan and Nelligan do not deny the importance that production as such, in the factory and on the assembly lines, still has. Yet, perhaps the most important aspect of this new and in some ways predominant mode of production is not as much the value of the commodity (as an external object) as it is that of the subjectivity being produced. The ambivalence of the creative dimension and value (and potential alienation) of this subjectivity is obvious; so are the common ground and univocal relationship among people active in completely different – perhaps apparently unrelated – sectors of the new economy. In *Border as Method* (2013), Mezzadra and Neilson consider the two figures of the care worker and the financial trader. They say, "These two groups of workers – carers and traders – occupy seemingly opposite ends of the world labor spectrum in terms of gender, earnings, and the relative assignment of bodily and cognitive tasks. But they are materially and symbolically linked within the global multiplication of labor" (112). Despite the important differences between the two groups of workers – most important of all, the obvious fact that "traders are an extremely privileged category of workers" (114) – just like migrant care workers, "traders sell not a predefined set of personality traits but their ability or potential to *become* the right person, the one required by their employers (or by the market) as circumstances change" (115). What is important is the stress on the creative, entrepreneurial injunction to become a certain subjectivity under conditions that – as Lordon (2014) also points out – are always conditions of capture, though the subjectivity of either the trader or the carer has a completely different position (different value) within the neoliberal economy. "The trader is," of course, "a particular kind of worker whose labor produces a subjectivity that is forever becoming a capitalist" (Mezzadra and Neilson 2013: 116). On the other hand, in any given society or community, migrant care workers always remain, to various degrees, at the margins of the economy and society, included as the excluded ones – an inclusion which is, as in the case of the total institutions like the prison, one of absolute capture. Moreover, Mezzadra and Neilson say with a reference to Anderson (2000), employers are in this case ultimately buying the whole body, "the whole person" of the worker (Anderson 2000, cited in Mezzadra and Neilson 109). Yet, Mezzadra and Neilson add, "The implicit threat on blackmail or even sabotage that haunts the payment of traders' bonuses is a reverse image of the reality of coercion produced by the combination of labor regulation, border, and visa regimes that apply to care workers and other less skilled migrants" (2013: 115). Importantly, however, in their recasting of the logic of inclusion and exclusion, Mezzadra and Neilson also say that the migrant worker, and in particular the "illegal" migrant "is not only subject to exclusion but also becomes a key actor in reshaping, contesting, and redefining the borders of citizenship" (257).

We have seen the importance of the production of subjectivity. As Mezzadra and Neilson say, "elaborating on Foucauldian terms ... subjectivity is a battleground, where multiple devices of subjection are confronted with practices of subjectivation" (2013: 252). This is central to the concept of subjectivity. On the one hand, we are subjected to power, the system, and so on. On the other, we have this power (and that is living labor as an ontological power) to become subjects, agents; the power to resist, fight back, and create something new. This living labor, labor power, is "precisely a form of power that exceeds, and in a certain sense precedes, processes of discipline and control, dispossession and exploitation" (264).[12] As Mezzadra and Neilson say, this "means to take seriously the two senses of the genitive in the phrase 'production of subjectivity'" (*ibid.*), and thus the twofold process of subjection and subjectivation. The subject is precisely the transindividual reality (a singularity) between subjection and subjectivation. Yet, a more radical concept of singularity is trans-dividuality, which absolutely exits the subject paradigm. Mezzadra and Neilson elaborate on these themes with important references to the work of Jacques Rancière, especially his notion of "the part of those who have no part" from *Dis-Agreement* (1998) – and they note how "it is easy to see that 'illegal' migrants are among the most obvious candidates to play the role of the part with no part" (2013: 254) – and the work of Étienne Balibar, among others. Of Balibar, they stress the link he establishes between *sovereignty* and *subjection* in the making of what then appears as the free individual (258) – but should really be, Balibar says, *the transindividual*, as we have seen above (Balibar 2014: 102–103). Yet, what is of particular importance in Mezzadra and Neilson's book for our discourse on art and labor is the idea that subjectivity cannot be completely determined, in a sovereign fashion, by techniques of subjection. In fact, subjectivity truly appears as and through the living modality of rupture, the exit from a situation of subjection, and the transforming – this time truly *creative* – project of subjectivation, or rather, to keep with Mezzadra and Neilson's conceptualization and terminology, of *multiplication*. It is this type of reality that I prefer to designate only as singularity. This is of course also the case in Hardt and Negri's *Assembly* (2017) as well as in many other authors dealing with these issues. In particular, Hardt and Negri completely reconceptualize the notion of the entrepreneur and speak of "entrepreneurship of the multitude" (2017: 139–150). One may be taken aback by this at first, for the entrepreneur seems to be a key figure of neoliberal ideology, and as Lazzarato (2012) correctly says, we live today under the injunction to become entrepreneurs of the self in the new debt economy. Hardt and Negri acknowledge that; yet, in a bold move, they say they "want to insist that first and foremost entrepreneurship belongs to the multitude, and names the multitude's capacities for cooperative social production and reproduction" (2017: 139). For them, this is not at all a way of updating our vocabulary and bringing it to match that of neoliberal ideology. To the contrary, as they argue, it is a way "to take . . . back and claim . . . as our own" words that have been "diverted and distorted" (*ibid.*) by capital and its ideology. This is certainly very relevant to what we were saying above about the concept of creativity, the word 'creative,' but also the figure of the artist in general. Indeed, as Morgan and Nelligan say, "capitalism's belated conversion to the gospel of creativity is profoundly ironic" (2018: Loc 534–539). This is a central point in the present chapter. The idea is not to succumb to subjection, but rather to subvert its conditions and undertake a project of transfiguration, transformation, and multiplication of singularities. In fact, what must be understood by the concept of multitude are not at all crowds of people, the "disunited multitude," which inspired fear in Hobbes (1994: 111), but rather, in light of the concept of trans-dividuality, singularities – an ensemble of singularities, as Negri says.[13]

In a similarly bold (and seemingly problematic) move, Mezzadra and Neilson recast the ideas of the border and No Border struggles in the context of the twofold process of subjection and subjectivation, and thus of the singularity of migrants. They say, "No Border struggles sometimes approach the border as an object to be eliminated rather than as a bundle of social relations that involve the active subjectivity of border crossers as much as the interdictory efforts of border police and other control agencies. This can give rise to a certain fixation on power and domination that paradoxically risks reinforcing the spectacle of the border" (2013: 267). They continue, "However, we do not think that the fabrication of the common always and in all circumstances requires or can reflect the elimination of borders" (279). For them, "it is the quality of the social relations that are constituted and reproduced by and through borders that matters" (*ibid.*). Just as in Hardt and Negri, the main question here is that of a transformative political project geared toward the production of new singularities and the construction of the common. For this, Mezzadra and Neilson note that it is important to understand "how the border is productive of subjectivity, rather than acting as a mere limit on already-formed subjects" (268). The production of subjectivity cuts across the whole spectrum of life and labor activities. This is so because ultimately the ontological power that living labor is constitutes the univocal ground of the social. Capital will continue to distinguish between productive and unproductive activities. It will also continue to completely overlook the importance of those reproductive activities without which no everyday life situation can sustain itself, let alone flourish and thrive. In this sense, housework, the work of care, attention, and affective labor in general, will continue to be undervalued, underpaid or totally unpaid, if acknowledged at all. The same is true of the genuinely creative activities (those of reproduction constituting an important part of them), which are marginalized as the idea of creativity becomes a catchword for the gig economy. The point is that artistic, creative labor is not what the neoliberal, gig economy says; and this is not so because artistic, creative labor is a type of activity reserved to the few engaging in established artistic fields, the fine arts, but rather because it covers a much larger spectrum of life activities, if not all of them, to various degrees. In particular, the rhythmic activities of social and everyday life, those of reproduction such as childcare work or the work of care in general, are inherently creative, and thus artistic. In fact, all life and labor activities can share in the creative, artistic modality – and they all do to various degrees, though often in a rather unacknowledged way. In this sense, the dimension of care is essential and it should be seen as a univocal, or transversal, modality of social relations – certainly informing laboring and artistic activities. Probably, it is easy to see how all art, all artistic activity, must have forms of care at its center and throughout. It might be more difficult to always see care as inherent in other life and work activities. Yet, this should not exclude those activities from sharing in the same paradigm of attention and care, which can perhaps be taken for granted when we think and speak about art. This would certainly be the case when the paradigm of social interaction is one of cooperation. Thus, if I can put it this way, care really is the middle term between art and labor. This means that care, including the care of the self, provides an exit from the logic of subjection and subsumption. In truth, through care, both art and labor return to themselves, to their original ontological (and ethical) disposition and power. It is in and through care – which involves the moments of desire and action – that subversion and exit become possible. But for this to be the case, care needs to be subtracted from the logic of capital and patriarchy and be given the dignity and status that really belongs to it. This is what in *Earthly Plenitudes* (Gullì 2010) I term *dignity of individuation*, which is the truth and justice of art and labor. The point is to see care as an ontological power for social transformation, which is essentially creative. Obviously, this is very far from the way in which neoliberal ideology uses words like creativity, art, and care. In fact, in the neoliberal economy the use and abuse of "the model of care," as Cristina Morini (2010),[14] among others, shows, have a completely different meaning. First of all, Morini highlights the "biopolitical dimension" that follows the transition from a Fordist to a post-Fordist mode of production. She calls the former "the age of measure (factory-based, rigid, stable, masculine)" and the latter "the age of quality (cognitive, relational, precarious, feminine)" (129).

This is the passage not only toward flexibility, but also toward affective labor and the feminization of labor (*ibid.*). In the neoliberal economy, the distinction between work and nonwork becomes thinner or altogether disappears (130). The concept of "care," Morini says (and here she puts the word in quotes), is instrumental to the "affirmation of the devastating sovereign logic of exchange value . . . that seeks to introduce ethics in the productive arena" (129). Morini says, *"The labor of care embodies the crisis of the measure of the value of labor today"* (132; emphasis in the original). In this sense, "women's 'unpaid work' (the labor of reproduction and care) becomes an interesting archetype of contemporary production" (*ibid.*). The same happens with the concept of creativity, adopted by capital and used for its own purposes and advantages. However, as Morgan and Nelligan say, "creativity has its roots in play and curiosity" (Loc 583). For capital, it becomes an organizing concept of a completely different kind. Yet, the point is that of translating or retranslating words and concepts in view of desired social changes and the struggle for them.

This is also a work of translation, of bringing over and across, of bringing forth something that is essentially different; it is transcendence within the plane of immanence. In my discussion of Theodor W. Adorno's *Aesthetic Theory* in the final chapter of *Labor of Fire*, I point out how for Adorno, first of all, "artistic labor is social labor" (Adorno 1997: 236). This means that creative or artistic labor is constitutive of society – it is part of labor's ontological power. Adorno says, "The immanence of society in the artworks is the essential social relation of art, not the immanence of art in society" (232). Yet in the network society, or what Boltanski and Chiapello call a *connexionist* world, made of links and ultimately networks, where a degree of democratization exists by default, the immanence of society in the artworks, or in the works of technology, necessarily means a reshaping of the living, sensuous (in Marx's sense)[15] aspect of things, of human subjectivity as it interacts with the nonhuman world in general, and with machines in particular. New singularities are thus formed, or produced, transversally, or trans-dividually, linked and intertwined *in* and *as* new machinic assemblages. However, the point is that under the current system of capital, which is, as Maurizio Lazzarato (2014) says, "an assemblage of assemblages" (46), singularities are lost in "individualization (subjection) and deindividualization (enslavement)" (*ibid.*). The alternative is then to build a politics of singularities, which is, to quote Lazzarato again, "a politics beyond the human" (125), given that the human is precisely this individualized and deindividualized (subjected and enslaved) entity.

An interesting point made by Hardt and Negri in *Assembly*, with a reference to Baruch Spinoza and Gilbert Simondon, is that "humans and machines belong to the same ontological plane" (2017: 110). Hardt and Negri use this insight to recast the notions of fixed capital, which is, they say quoting Marx from the *Grundrisse*, "man himself" (Marx 1973: 712;

Hardt and Negri 2017: 115), and the composition of capital. Today, obviously, the question of the machine has to be seen not only in terms of mechanization and automation, but also, and perhaps particularly, in terms of digitization. Thus, algorithms are part of this discourse. Hardt and Negri say that an algorithm "is fixed capital, a machine that is born of social, cooperative intelligence, a product of 'general intellect,' . . . [which has] the power of living labor" as its foundation (118). They stress that "without living labor there is no algorithm" (*ibid.*). It is in this sense that there is always a trans-dividual structure (and ontology) in the *machinic*, which "never refers to an individual, isolated machine but always an assemblage" (121). Interestingly, Hardt and Negri point out the difference between the multitude and the machinic assemblage: the former is understood "exclusively in terms of human singularities"; the latter is "composed of a wider range of beings, human and nonhuman" (122). They are both important for a discourse on art and labor today, and certainly the notion of a machinic assemblage is crucial, for it highlights the new poetic ontology, and the poetic experience, of the present. It is now no longer a question of being an appendage to the machine, thus of alienation. As Gerald Raunig (2016) says, "Future machinic environments might be more readily conceived in terms of the logic of enveloping than of appending or physically touching" (112). The cloud replaces the appendage. Raunig speaks of "an endless (self-) enveloping of every single person" (113). The main modality is that of "Self-assembling and assembling the assemblage" (114). Above I spoke about a new poetic ontology and a new poetic experience; they still retain a dimension of *danger*. Yet, the experience remains one of freedom (as indeterminacy) and the production of being. Indeed, with the notion of enveloping – still a trans-dividual notion – we are back to the idea of the border as a site of production of subjectivities, or singularities. As Jean-Luc Nancy says in *The Experience of Freedom* (1993), the experience of freedom, as "the experience of experience," or "experience itself," is precisely "trying the self at the self's border," and in this sense it is "the passage of limit" (87). It is "the *peril of the crossed limit*" (*ibid.*). In fact, as Peter Fenves notes, in his foreword to *The Experience of Freedom*, "The word 'experience,' as Nancy reminds us, once had the sense of a perilous traversing (*peirō*) of the limit (*peras*)" (xx). As Nancy says, this experience is "existence – rather than the experience *of* existence" (89). The self, even in the machinic assemblage (and particularly so), which is always at the intersection of art and labor, *poiesis* and *praxis*, is also always trans-dividual. Existence, Nancy says, is always coexistence, being-with. Indeed, being is always being-with. As he says in a highly suggestive sentence, "To exist is a matter of going into exile" (78). We find the border again, the conceptual and actual overlapping of the border and the threshold, and the unrest and potency inherent in the production of ever-new singularities.

NOTES

1. This chapter is a shortened and revised version of Gullì, Bruno. "Dis/Art, (This) Labor: Transfigurations in the Age of Precarity and Disposability," which appeared in *Parse*, Issue 9, Spring 2019.
2. See Mezzadra and Neilson (2013) and Gullì (2014).
3. For the concept of transindividuation, see Jason Read (2016), *The Politics of Transindividuality*.
4. For the notions of being-with and the singular plural, see Nancy (2000).
5. See my discussion of the points in Gullì (2005).
6. See Lazzarato (2012), *The Making of the Indebted Man*.
7. On this point, also see Hardt and Negri's important analysis (2017: 173).
8. See Federici (2012) and Dalla Costa and James (1972).
9. See my discussion of this point in Chapter Four of *Earthly Plenitudes* (Gullì 2010).
10. See Hardt and Negri's remark on whiteness (53).
11. See my discussion in Chapter Four of *Labor of Fire* (Gullì 2005).
12. See also my discussion of living labor as an ontological power in Gullì (2005).
13. In relation to the *Gilets Jaunes* movement in France, Negri has recently spoken of a passage to class of an otherwise dispersed multitude.
14. The translation of all passages from Morini's book is mine.
15. See Marx's *Theses on Feuerbach* (Marx 1975a: 421).

EIGHT

Disaffection and Care

In *A Grammar of the Multitude*, Paolo Virno (2004) says that singularities should be considered "as a point of arrival, not as a starting point; as the ultimate result of a *process of individuation*, not as solipsistic atoms" (76). Here we see again the distance from Leibniz's monad, and the similarity to Guattari's account of the dynamic modality of the singular, but it is also an accurate rendering of Simondon's notion of individuation as an ongoing, never completed, process. Virno also calls into question the notion of the individual, which is always to be understood from within the multitude, as "the final stage of a process beyond which there is nothing else" (*ibid.*) in the sense that there is no One, but Many, the multitude, "a network of *individuals*," in other words, a singularity made of a multiplicity of singularities. What precedes individuation itself is, Virno says, "a *pre-individual reality*, that is to say, something common, universal and undifferentiated" (*ibid.*).[1] But in reality what comes with individuation is not the individual as such, but the trans-dividual as an open singularity. In fact, beyond the fictitious individual, its apparent finitude, the true finitude of singularity trespasses into the region of the infinitizing threshold, the measure of the incompleteness of individuation.

We have seen in Chapter Two how important it is for Simondon to think of the *relative* individual and in fact even of the possibility of "replacing the individual in being" (Simondon 2013: 32). This has to do with the notion of being that Simondon puts forth, as he himself notes. According to this notion, "being has no unity of identity, which is that of the stable state within which no transformation is possible" (31); instead, "being has a transductive unity" whereby "it can phase-shift in relation to itself [*il peut se déphaser par rapport à lui-même*]" (*ibid.*). Simondon also says, "The individuated being is neither the whole being nor the primary being" (*ibid.*). And: "Individuation must be grasped as the becoming of being, and not as a model of being that exhausted its signification" (*ibid.*); that is, that exhausted its potential, or its pre-individual reserve. Contrary to the apparent anti-Parmenidean aspect of this, in truth Parmenides himself allows for the potential within the real, for that which is must be the same as that for which there is thought; moreover, perhaps more essentially, what-is is because it can be. But what is important here, particularly in relation to Virno's reading of this Simondonian point, is that "rather than grasping individuation starting from the individuated being, we must grasp the individuated being starting from individuation, and individuation starting from pre-individual being" (31–32).

For Virno, "individuality is the final product of a process of individuation which stems from the universal, the generic, the pre-individual" (2004: 76). In truth, this is not entirely accurate since the process of individuation, as Virno himself explicitly says later, is never really completed, and thus individuality remains something like a mirage. The figure within the multitude is not that of the individual, but of the singular. It is in this sense that the notion of the multitude radically differs from liberal thought, and not in the sense that it values individuality albeit in a different way, as Virno claims. Singularity, a wider reality than individuality, does not exhibit the latter's separation, independence, and distance. It certainly makes no claims to sovereignty. The multitude is within the singular just like the singular is within the multitude. In order to get to the multitude, one does not need many singularities: singularity as such is already plural, what seems to be one is already many. This is something that individuality, caught within itself, its independence and sovereignty, can never achieve. There is no way that individuality and singularity can be reconciled. Singularity is trans-dividual in a way that individuality, by definition, cannot be. It is in this sense that we can understand Virno's claim that pre-individual reality, which is "essentially *historical*" (77) is also the dimension of "the prevailing relation of production" (*ibid.*). Virno makes here an important reference to Marx's concept of the *general intellect*, which is precisely this pre-individual reality. He says, "The contemporary multitude is composed of individualized individuals, who have behind them also *this* pre-individual reality" (78). It is here that Virno, going back to Simondon, repeats what we already saw in Chapter Two, dealing with another of his works, that "*individuation is never concluded*" and, he adds, that "the pre-individual is never fully translated into singularity" (*ibid.*; original emphasis). The incompleteness of individuation is something that we have sufficiently focused on. The remainder of the pre-individual, its not fully passing into singularity, is a statement about the reserve of potentiality and the idea that pre-individual reality is not a chronological first that yields to something (a second or third, and so on) other than itself, but rather the fabric of the structuring ontology of the common, immanent within the singular. Virno also points out and explains Simondon's concept of the *subject*, to which we will return in the next chapter. He says that for Simondon the subject "consists of the permanent interweaving of pre-individual elements and individuated characteristics; moreover, the subject *is* this interweaving" (*ibid.*). Virno also warns that it "would be a serious mistake, according to Simondon, to identify the subject with one of its components, the one which is singularized" (*ibid.*), or rather, we should say, individualized, for singular and individual are completely different concepts. As I anticipated in Chapter Six, above, Virno says, "The subject is a battlefield" (*ibid.*). Perhaps we can add that it is a battlefield of relations, and we will see the importance of the notion of relation for Simondon, as he treats precisely of the subject, in the next and final chapter. For now, I just want to note that this ensemble of relations is also what Virno calls the multitude. As he says, "the combination of 'social individuals' [is] the multitude" (80). He also says, "The individual is *social* because within the individual the general intellect is present" (*ibid.*; original emphasis). Yet, drawing different conclusions from Virno's, I would say that Marx's theory around the *social individual* and the *general intellect* is not at all "a rigorous individualism" (*ibid.*), or simply "a theory of individuation" (*ibid.*), but rather a theory of psychic and collective individuation (which can scarcely be called an individualism), a theory of trans-dividuation, an opening into the "internal resonance" of transduction, whereby the 'individual' becomes "a node of informative communication," "a system within a system" (Simondon 2005: 28). Indeed, the social individual is precisely no longer an individual, but the dividual at the threshold of otherness and trans-dividuality. Otherwise, this undoes the concept of the multitude. It is then of singularity rather than individuality that we are speaking. And it is precisely this being at the threshold that opens up, for what seems to be an individual, the possibility and danger of disindividuation, as we will soon see with Stiegler. It is true that Simondon uses the word 'individual' in this context, but he complicates it insofar as, with respect to the living being at least, "individuation happens inside," through internal resonance (*ibid.*). As Simondon moves from form to information, from the hylemorphic to the transductive paradigm, he sees that the transindividual corresponds to "the obscure zone" of the hylemorphic scheme, which must be overcome. As he says, "the hylemorphic scheme . . . impedes the knowledge of *ontogenesis*" (303), that is, the genesis of the real. This is the obscure zone that hides the truth of transindividuality, of the thresholds and gathering, of what does away with the fiction of the individual. This is what we call the singular, or singularity.

The loss of the potentiality of pre-individual reality and of the horizon of transindividuality can be understood as disindividuation. Bernard Stiegler (2010) says that for Simondon, the proletarian "is a *disindividuated* worker, a laborer whose knowledge has passed into the machine in such a way that it is no longer the worker who is individuated through bearing tools and putting them into practice" (37). In other words, proletariazation is a *"loss of savoir-faire"* (33; original emphasis). Stiegler says that the disindividuated laborer is not, precisely, "co-individuated" in technical (and machinic, we can add) individuation, but that it simply "does not ex-ist" (*ibid*), where the hyphenated word is a reminder of the phenomenological and existential understanding of the concept of existence as an ecstatic standing out. Differently from Virno's emphasis on the *general intellect* and the producer, in Stiegler proletarianization "excludes [the] participation of the producer from the evolution of the conditions of production" (38). The loss of *savoir-faire* of producers corresponds to the loss of the *savoir-vivre* of consumers, who are disindividuated, for consumption is a form of intoxication (2013: 83). This is what Stiegler calls "generalized proletarianization" (3) and *"generalized disaffection"* (87), a consequence of *"affective saturation"* (86). For Stiegler, this is part of the current crisis that takes on the form of *spiritual misery* and *systemic stupidity*. For him, we live in "the *reign or kingdom of stupidity* [*règne de la bêtise*]" (4). One is of course bound to agree with Stiegler's powerful and adequate analysis of the present, especially when one looks at the performance of so-called world leaders today, but also at the present lack of cultural depth in society, the lack of attention, and the crisis of what Stiegler, partly with Simondonian language, calls "psychic *and* collective (cerebral and social)" individuation (2). What is interesting, however, is that for Stiegler this dystopic situation created by capitalism is also what ultimately threatens capitalism itself (5). It is from this dystopia that a kind of *plasticity* unfolds, a trans-formation and a passage (a threshold) to a possible heterotopia, an alternative space, in the sense of Foucault.

Stiegler focuses on the two moments of *disaffection* [*désaffection*] and *withdrawal* or *disaffectation* [*désaffectation*]. Both of them disturbances, the former is the loss of *psychic* individuation; the latter is the loss of *social* or *collective* individuation (90). The two are connected through the generalized loss of attention typical of the society of digital technology and control, which "engenders ... disaffection [*désaffection*], ruining [people's] affective capacities; and it engenders their withdrawal [*désaffectation*], the loss of their place, that is of their ethos" (7; brackets added). Obviously, this is a reference to Heidegger's great interpretation of Heraclitus's saying, *ēthos anthrōpōi daimōn* in *Letter on Humanism* (1977a: 233). For Heidegger this statement means that the dwelling place or abode (*ēthos*) of human beings is "in the nearness of god," an "open region" (*ibid*.), and thus, a threshold. For Stiegler, ethics is precisely "the knowledge of the *abode* [*séjour*]" (2013: 7). *Ēthos* is "that which gives me my *place* within the *circuit of affects* through which the process of psychic and collective individuation constitutes itself" (8). Disaffection and withdrawal are the loss of *ēthos* in this sense. Stiegler describes this "appalling reality of spiritual misery" as a "loss of consciousness and affect, induced by cognitive and affective saturation" (90), and he says that it "characterizes the *lost spirit of capitalism*" (*ibid*.). Ultimately, but only in a sense, it is a matter of capitalism destroying itself. Stiegler's language is here very powerful: "Today there are disaffected people just as there are disused factories [*usines désaffectées*]: there are human wastelands just as there are industrial wastelands" (*ibid.*). It is like a war that has, to use Ken Saro-Wiwa's wonderful expression, *uselessed* so many people (Saro-Wiwa 1994). This situation calls into question the possibility of transindividuality as it transforms control societies into "unliveable societies of disaffected individuals, that is, uncontrollable individuals" (Stiegler 2013: 8). For Stiegler, the exit from this situation is *care*, which, he says, is the same as *spirit* [*esprit*], or the Greek *nous*, thought. He says that the noetic or spiritual dimension of human beings is intermittent in its actual phase as human beings themselves "ceaselessly oscillate between the *desire for taming* and the *temptation of fury*" (10). Stiegler does not believe that humanity can be domesticated, but rather that it finds itself at the threshold indicated above, the oscillation or vacillation between those two extremes. Stiegler's idea of taming should not be understood in the Nietzschean sense, but rather in the sense that, as Stiegler eloquently says, "humans carry within themselves a savagery that they trans-form into singularity" (*ibid.*). He adds that "this singularity is a potential for socialization" (*ibid.*). What is at stake here is the failure of control societies, which, Stiegler says, "are not sustainable" and only bring about the reign of stupidity and misery (11). But ultimately they are not sustainable because at bottom, that is, pre-individually and potentially, human beings are uncontrollable. This is the meaning of Stiegler's important questions, "How could it be . . . that control societies are not domesticated societies? How is it that this 'control' fails to make possible the *submission* of the human beast?" (*ibid.*). Stiegler says, "The answer is that when human beings are controlled, and when this control deprives them of their desire, that is, their singularity, they become bestial and furious, in the sense that their drives are unleashed, until eventually they become radically uncontrollable" (*ibid.*).

Singularity is another word for care, and it is the opposite of misery and stupidity. I have already noted that singularity is love. It is the opposite of disindividuation and disaffection. However, that does not mean that it is the same as individuality, not even individuation. Singularity is the nondenumerable and what escapes seriality. The hope of uncontrollable individuals, who are really fragments of dividuality, is the singular, the expression of the common. The question is whether the singular is today possible at all. Perhaps it is if what is uncontrollable destroys the machinery of control: the State, the bureaucracy, the police, the logic of normalization, and, as Stiegler has it, the reign of misery and stupidity. Obviously, given the contingency of all this, the contingency of history, this is not impossible. Antagonistic struggle is care, and care is ethos, namely, dwelling at the threshold of the common gathering. It is, as Stiegler says, spirit and *nous*, thought. Indeed, the main – though contingent – struggles, a plurality of struggles, are against thoughtlessness and stupidity. But struggle is also a matter of technics, an important concept in Stiegler, just as control and subjection (submission and subjugation) operate through technics. Technics of servitude do their best to control, subject, subjugate, and submit, and yet they are ultimately bound to fail. Technics of liberation spring up at innumerable thresholds, for what is "disquieting, terrifying, monstrous, or marvelous," as Stiegler reminds us of with an apt reference to Sophocles' *Antigone* (Stiegler 2013: 10), the human being, is uncontrollable, yet capable of care and singularization, expressing the character of the common. The question of technics of servitude is very important. I am currently collaborating with Peter Bratsis and Michael Pelias, of The Institute for the Radical Imagination, on a book project that deals precisely with that question: Why is it that, in liberal and neoliberal societies, so many people seem to prefer servitude to freedom? Moreover, what are the technics of enslavement? Frédéric Lordon (2014) has demonstrated very clearly how what may appear as voluntary servitude is always *passionate* servitude, and I have dealt with aspects of his work in the present book. With Stiegler we now see that this systematic and systemic attempt at controlling and enslaving is bound to fail, that it certainly never fully succeeds. Essentially, what is uncontrollable in the human condition, the human adventure, is much wider, ontologically deeper and stronger, than whatever any national or global security algorithm is able to control. Moreover, if machinic enslavement is a sad and appalling reality and the algorithm is often that of capital, there can also be an algorithm of liberation and the construction, through the machine, through technē, of a trans-dividual reality, a new ethos in the spirit of *ubuntu*, the wonderful concept from the philosophical tradition of Southern Africa describing humanity as being-with, care, a matter of relations, relations of relations, "I am because we are."

In an interesting elaboration on Deleuze and Guattari's notion of *machinic*, in the context of a discussion of Marx's chapter on machines in Volume I of *Capital* and the so-called "Fragment on Machines" in the *Grundrisse*, but more generally a discussion of the relationship between living labor / living knowledge and machines, Matteo Pasquinelli (2014) says that 'machinic' indicates more than the instrumentality of the assemblage, to which it is often reduced. Instead, for Pasquinelli, the etymology of *machinic*, the Latin *machina* and the Ancient Greek *mechané*, points to a surplus and to amplification (89). He points out that the root *mach-* "in various Indo-European languages means growth, increment, amplification of force" (*ibid.*). He says that the same root is also present in the Latin words *magia* and *magnus*, and he references the German *Macht*, which means power, potency (*ibid.*). Pasquinelli concludes, "In other words, when Deleuze and Guattari spoke of *machinic surplus-value*, they were simply making the ancient root of the word 'machine' resonate" (*ibid.*). Thus, for Pasquinelli there is *more* in 'machine' than in words like 'instrument,' 'dispositif,' or 'medium.' The former is "an apparatus for the amplification and accumulation of a given flux" of energy, labor, information, and so on; the latter would be responsible "for the translation and extension of such a flux" (*ibid.*). This is different from the notion of machinic assemblage we have seen in the previous chapter, a notion worked upon by Gerald Raunig and others. In fact, Pasquinelli mentions Raunig in this respect, in particular his book *A Thousand Machines* (2010). From the bicycle in Vittorio de Sica's *Bicycle Thieves*, a radical adaptation of Luigi Bartolini's novel *Ladri di biciclette*, to Deleuze and Guattari's abstract machines, passing through Marx's so-called "Fragment on Machines," Raunig interprets the notion of machine in a way that is not entirely different from Pasquinelli's intriguing remark about its etymology. Indeed, the potency and amplification of force belongs in the machinic assemblage, which is precisely *more* than each (or all) of its constituent parts. Trans-dividuality, or singularity, is precisely this *more*, whether one thinks of it in the strictly machinic sense or not. Raunig also addresses the same etymological point we have seen in Pasquinelli. He says, precisely, that "the Greek *mechané* and the Latin *machina* prove to belong to the etymological line of the hypothetical Indo-European root **magh-*, which is probably related to the old Indian *maghá* and the Iranian *magu-*, referring to the semantic field of 'power, force, capacity'" (105). And he also references the German *Macht* ('power'), just as Pasquinelli does. For Raunig, the point is to understand that the machinic mode (etymologically understood), should be initially seen, outside the paradigm of domination, and following Foucault, as a relation of forces (*ibid.*). Outside the paradigm of domination also means outside the metaphysics of subjectivity, the subject, and the obsolete subject/object formula. Raunig says, "In this sense the machine is not the means of a powerful subject, which thus accomplishes its metabolic exchange with nature, but rather a differential relationship, an assemblage that provides impulses for specific modes of subjectivation" (105–106). In this book, we have also abandoned subjectivation as an exit from subjection and capture, and we have instead presented singularization as a more adequate modality of the threshold and immanent expression of the common. With this in mind, we can agree with Pasquinelli's notion of amplification of force as well as with Raunig's understanding of the machinic assemblage as a power, which he says, "following Spinoza," should be understood "*before* any stratification, appropriation and instrumentalization as potency, capability and possibility" (106). In other words, the *more*, or surplus, of machinic assemblage is one of singularity, love, and care.

At the outset of Part 3 of his *Ethics*, which is about the origin and nature of the emotions, Spinoza says that the emotions should be considered as "natural phenomena that follow the laws of Nature," not as "phenomena outside Nature" (1992: 102). This is another way of reminding us of the paradigm of immanence and the "God, or Nature" truth. Based on the emotions as natural phenomena, ethos and care are also natural and material occurrences. Ethos defines one's dwelling place, and care is the proper way of handling or managing it. Care is concrete and material not only when it is hands-on care, but in general. As an affective, emotional, and ethical attitude, care is a set of technics, as well as the spirit, of attention. The act of attention, which overcomes disaffection and produces care, is made possible by the disposition and orientation of preindividual reality, that is, of the affects, by desire. It is a phenomenon or event of the threshold, for, as Paul Ricoeur (2016) says, its essential character is that of the question and of the exploration (36). With a reference to Edmund Husserl, Ricoeur says that it is a matter of *turning toward* or *turning away*, and he calls this "the specific distribution of the field of attention" (*ibid.*). But this exploration or question tries to individuate, and, insofar as it is active (rather than passive) attention, to take care of the being, the object, the situation or "landscape" (Ricoeur says) whose *aspect* has changed, but whose *meaning* has remained the same (30). Attention makes possible "the apprehension of a new aspect that was not perceived as an aspect" (31). In this sense, it changes the *ethos*, the open abode, and it engenders the modality of care. Insofar as attention "makes us masters of our actions," as Ricoeur says (43), it also signals, and makes possible, the passage from *human bondage* to *human freedom*, to use Spinoza's expressions in Part IV and Part V of the *Ethics*. Attention, and the ensuing mode of care, can then be seen as the technic, "the method, or way, leading to freedom" (Spinoza 1992: 201). This is also a passage from necessity to contingency, the ability to give a new orientation to preindividual reality and cross the threshold of the trans-dividual gathering, which is a multitudinous and collective assembling, an assemblage, or amplification of force. It would perhaps be a return from disindividuation, for as Stiegler says, the lack of attention, or *toxicomania* as a social model, is "a form of control that has given up on any psychic and collective individuation" (2013: 102; emphasis removed). Given his focus on the question of youth, consumption, and the future ethos, Stiegler also adds that "the attention deficit comes from society, a society which nevertheless, blames the children who suffer because of it and to whom it is not attentive, and a society which, at the same time, captures and channels attention onto objects of consumption" (*ibid.*). The opposition between the two moments, or models, of disaffection/disindividuation and ethos/care is perhaps one of the most important issues of our time. The critique of the paradigm of subjectivity and individuality, the abandonment of the logic of number, which is not simply a theoretical endeavor but a political, practical struggle as well, can show the way for the transition to the open determination (not a closed determinateness) of singularity, the threshold of the common, which may take the shape of a movement of return, and yet it is also the passage to what is other, otherness as such. Number, as Hegel (1995) says, for instance in his treatment of the Pythagoreans in the first volume of his *Lectures on the History of Philosophy*, are completely devoid of the Notion, that is, of *logos* and thus of the singular and common – for that is what *logos* (the gathering threshold, as we will see in a moment with Heidegger) is. As Hegel says, the various determinations of number, after the number one, "are only further combinations and repetitions of the one, which all through remains fixed and external; number, thus, is the most utterly dead, notionless continuity possible"; it is, he continues, "an entirely external and mechanical process" (210). To be sure, despite some criticism of the Pythagorean tradition, Hegel does say that "the Pythagoreans did not accept numbers in this indifferent way, but as Notion" (*ibid.*), thus – at least that was apparently the intention – as logos and thought, as universal ideas – though numbers remained midway between the sensuous and thought, Hegel adds. But numbers as such, certainly the way they are used as an instrument in today's control society, remain precisely the same as Hegel says, "the most worthless instruments for expressing Notion-determinations" (*ibid.*). We understand Hegel's expression "Notion-determinations" as singularities, that is, the movement of thought and the process of individuation whereby trans-dividual relations become effective and relevant. Otherwise, and here Hegel is criticizing some tendencies within the Pythagoreans as well, with numbers "everything came into indefinite and insipid relations in which the Notion disappeared" (228). Indeed, in a way that might also indicate a critique of modern positivistic thinking, Hegel also says that "numbers are dry forms and barren principles in which life and movement are deficient" (237).

Different from the logic and politics of number, more than simply opposed to it, is the modality of singularity, with which this book is concerned and which rests on the common gathering of attention and care. In his reading of "The Anaximander Fragment," Heidegger (1975) addresses the question of singularity and care in a very important way. Heidegger offers a new translation of a segment of the fragment about Anaximander, which usually reads, "The things that are perish into the things from which they come to be, according to necessity, for they pay penalty and retribution for their injustice in accordance with the ordering of time" (Curd 2011: 17). Heidegger is especially interested in correcting the translation of the Greek τὸ χρεών, usually translated as "necessity," and translates it as "usage." He also translates τίσις, usually rendered as "penalty," with the word "reck" (care). One segment of the fragment then says that things change "along the lines of usage; for they let order and thereby also reck [care] belong to one another (in the surmounting) of disorder" (Heidegger 1975: 57; brackets added). He says that τίσις is "esteem" and that to "esteem something means to heed it, and so to take satisfactory care of what is estimable in it" (45). But care is also part of the meaning of the word "usage," τὸ χρεών, for, as Heidegger shows by way of etymology, the word entails the idea of the hand (51), which is obviously essential in attention and care. For him, τὸ χρεών, as "usage," is "the handing over of presence," thus an act of attention and care, and that which "keeps in hand . . . what is present as such" (52). The careful user, or caring person, *persona carans*, to use an expression by Diemut Elizabeth Bubeck (1995: 12), is the antithesis of the disaffected and disindividuated individual. Indeed, for Bubeck, *"persona carans* could replace *homo economicus* as the individual theorized in social and political theory" (*ibid.*), in a way that would address the problematic, unhealthy rift between production and consumption. The concept of usage, or use, is important in many alternative (heterotopic) traditions, from Buddhism and Taoism to some forms of Christianity, such as the Franciscan tradition, to communism and anarchism. The idea of using without possessing occurs often in the *Daodejing*, for instance. But it is in usage that attention and care become essential, not in possessing. In fact, possessing is based on the pretension of security, namely, according to the etymology of the word from Latin, the condition of being free from care (*sine cura*, without care), and thus a total lack of care, total carelessness. Moreover, in the logic of security, just as care is replaced by carelessness, attention is replaced by violence and arrogance.

In *Being and Time*, Heidegger defines care as the fundamental structure of being-in-the-world in the specific mode of being-together-with and, precisely, *taking care* of things (1996b: 180). Care is thus the fundamental ethos, the abode, ontologically prior, in its structural totality, to the division between theoretical and practical endeavors, authentic and inauthentic possibilities, and so on. Essentially, care is, for humans, the time between birth and death, the meaning and structure of their *"temporal sojourn in the world"* (185). Heidegger illustrates this condition through the fable by Hyginus about "Care" (Cura) shaping the first human being. Heidegger calls this a pre-ontological illustration of the meaning of care. As there was a dispute among Jupiter, Earth, and Care itself as to who would own the human being, Saturn ("time") made the following decision: "Since you, Jupiter, have given its spirit, you should receive that spirit at death; and since you, Earth, have given its body, you shall receive its body. But since 'Care' first shaped this creature, she shall possess it as long as it lives" (184). It is interesting that, even in this pre-ontological account, this happens "in accordance with the ordering of time," just as one reads in the Anaximander Fragment. Equally interesting and important is that care appears here also as labor (broadly construed). It is not simply the labor of care in its practical specificity, the labor required through daily life, or even the labor that then becomes alienated and alienating, disaffecting and disindividuating, wage labor, "women's labor," or endless work in the 24/7 economy. It is rather all type of making and doing, the anxiety and restlessness defining, to go back to Stiegler, what is uncontrollable in the human condition. The act of taking care is the gathering of attention and care itself, and a constant struggle. It is not an attempt to control the uncontrollable – as the control societies try but necessarily fail to do, as Stiegler says; it is rather a way of shaping its possibilities. What requires the attention and direction (the shaping) of care is the uncontrollable, which cannot be dealt with by ever greater or more sophisticated forms and means of violence. The recent social unrest in many areas of the world from Europe to the Middle East, from Africa to South America, Far East Asia, and so on, precisely shows the power of the structure of care within the uncontrollable. In fact, care, in addition to being the fundamental ontological structure of being-in-the-world, as Heidegger says, is also essentially struggle. In truth, these two senses of the meaning of care come together when one thinks of it as defining the material conditions of existence, and, consequently, the facts of deficiency (lack) and dependency. In Chapter One, above, with a reference to the work of Arnold Gehlen's philosophical anthropology, we saw the importance of the original deficiency or lack that defines the human condition, thus the need for the making of tools, for technology. The fact of dependency is obviously linked to that original condition of deficiency, and it becomes fundamental in questions of political and social ontology dealing with attention and care, with the meaning and truth of trans-dividuality, namely, the threshold-like relation between the singular and the common – which is what is traditionally understood as the relation between the individuals and society.

In the previous chapter, we have anticipated some of the main aspects of care, especially in relation to the labor of care, from a feminist and migration studies perspective. We should now consider in particular the question of the relationship between dependency and care. In *Love's Labor: Essays on Women, Equality, and Dependency*, Eva Kittay says, "Dependents require care" (1). This is the very first sentence in her book. However, what she then shows is that dependency is "the inescapable fact" (16) of the human condition, and hence that the idea of the fully independent individual is largely a fiction. Everybody experiences dependency in their life. Newborns, elderly people in their fragility, even those who get to old age in relatively good health, people who have had a serious accident or illness (such as a stroke, and so on), and people with severe mental and/or physical disabilities spanning the time from birth to death, all require degrees of care due to their absolute or relative dependency as well as to their vulnerability. But dependency and the requirement of care also create a situation of general interdependence in the sense that the carer and the cared-for become part of a new relationship, an assemblage or network, we might say using the language we have seen before in the course of this book. This interdependence has the character of singularity, or trans-dividuality. Especially when the degree of dependency is very high or absolute, the modality of interdependence or transdependence, the trans-dividual relationship established by the requirement of care, materializes as the place and time of a gathering threshold, which is both an affirmation of the singular and a passage to the common. It has the form of a neither/nor of personhood: neither simply you nor simply I, but, in the sense of the notion of *ubuntu* we have seen above, the meaning of the self in the other and of the other, no longer in the self, which has in fact disappeared, but in its other. Obviously, there is here a danger, as in every crossing of the limit – a danger that should not be taken lightly. And yet, it is an unavoidable danger, which must be faced and entered into. The limit becomes a threshold, where the gathering happens and relations of power as power-to, not power-over, as potency ('amplification of force' and ability), not authority or domination, can be established whereby access to the possibility of the good life (or a decent life, at least), taken away or reduced by dependency can be restored, fully or to some degree. This is what creates communities, not the thoughtless imposition of external laws. This is where the singular meets the common, a prefiguration of relations without a subject. It is then not a matter of deciding between egotism and altruism, a useless and false dilemma of a long tradition of political and social thought. It is rather a matter of understanding that the constitution of whatever we call a 'self,' an 'individual,' is plural and trans-dividual and that it always has care as the locus of its gathering threshold. In other words, this 'amplification of force' would allow people, who otherwise would be excluded from it, to exercise "the whole range of capabilities" (Nussbaum 2006: 146) without which it is difficult to uphold dignity and guarantee flourishing. The "capabilities approach," developed by Martha Nussbaum in philosophy and by Amartya Sen in economics (70), begins with "a conception of the dignity of the human being, and of a life that is worthy of that dignity – a life that has available in it 'truly human functioning,' in the sense described by Marx in his 1844 *Economic and Philosophical Manuscripts*" (74). Although this might seem to be a concern of the individual, it does indeed have a trans-dividual character, for the "human functioning" (a Marxian and Aristotelian concept) is only found at the social level of being-with. Moreover, the ten central human capabilities developed by Nussbaum (76–78) have a universal, common, and trans-dividual importance. Singularities will be able to exercise them only insofar as the structuring modality of the common is in place. So, consider, for instance, the first capability in the list given by Nussbaum, '*Life*': "Being able to live to the end of a human life of normal length; not dying prematurely, or before one's life is so reduced as to be not worth living" (76). This is obviously nor simply an individual task, endeavor, or responsibility. Without the others, the trans-dividual network, an 'individual' will not be able to succeed in exercising this capability. This is even more immediately evident with other capabilities, which are more evidently trans-dividual in character. For instance, capability #5, '*Emotions*,' which addresses the importance of having "attachments to things and people outside ourselves" (*ibid.*); capability #8, '*Other Species*': "Being able to live with concern for and in relation to animals, plants, and the world of nature" (77); or capability #9, *'Play,'* which focuses on the ability to laugh, play, and enjoy recreational activities – all things that require a structure of being-with and entail the reality of the threshold. All the other capabilities have the same character, and they point out the importance of being-with, of the trans-dividual singularization of the common, the neutralization of the stifling politics of number (social atomism and existential alienation), and the meaning of attention and care as antidotes to disaffection.

In this chapter we have seen the play between disaffection and care, their dialectical relationship. In the next chapter we will see how the problematization of identity may foreshadow the paradigm of a subjectless network of relations, that is, the trans-dividual and singular difference constantly individuating, in a constant state of vacillation, at gathering thresholds.

NOTE

1. In the next chapter, we will see that for Nishida Kitarō, "the self can be thought from the depths of the world" (2012: 84). This relates to the concept of the multitude and of trans-dividuality. Virno also speaks of pre-individuality as "essentially *historical*" (2004: 77). Nishida says, "Our selves come into being from the depths of the historical world" (87).

NINE
Relations without a Subject

In a lecture on the concept of identity, Paul Ricoeur (2016) proposes three paradoxes that might help clarify the problematic nature of that concept. The first paradox has to do with the temporal structure of identity, the second with the relation between self and others, and the third with the related questions of responsibility and fragility. Ricoeur begins by distinguishing between *numeric* identity as repetition of the same, "ontogenetic (or developmental) identity of the same living thing from birth to death" (243) – which is really what the question of individuation is also about – and identity of *structure*, such as one's genetic code, and so on. He further distinguishes between *idem*-identity or sameness and *ipse*-identity or *ipseity*. Things in general are defined only by the former type of identity, which is a numeric, substantial, and structural identity – in other words, they are only defined in relation to the question *what*. The human being, on the other hand, is defined by both types of identity, and this is the paradox. Ricoeur says, "We must not say that things are on the side of sameness and persons on that of *ipseity*. Persons are on both sides" (*ibid.*). For Ricoeur, the important question is that of "the self-constancy of the *ipse*" (245), which indicates the '*who*' rather than '*what*' with respect to the human being. The danger would be that of "an ipseity without sameness" (246), unable to answer the question, Who am I? Obviously, the question raised by Ricoeur is very important. In the present work, following Simondon, then Deleuze and Guattari, as well as others, we have stressed the relative (or fictional) reality of the individual, and we have actually claimed that the individual as such does not exist and the self itself is a fictional construct. However, as Gerald Raunig (2016) points out, this does not mean that the dividual exists instead of the individual and that we are left with unrelated and scattered fragments of dividuality. In fact, the trans-dividual gathering has been proposed as, not simply a replacement for the individual, but more importantly as the meaning of the singular, constantly constituting itself at the threshold of the common. In this sense, singularity satisfies the requirements of Ricoeur's concept of ipseity. The time paradox presented by Ricoeur actually has a Heraclitean dimension, "We step into and we do not step into the same rivers. We are and we are not" (Curd 2011: 45). We are *no longer* what we used to be and *not yet* what we will be. However, this double 'not,' the no longer of the past and the not yet of the future, represents the dialectical and ontological constitution (or trans-stitution) of what, precisely, we are and are not. This does not mean that we have become, or will become, completely different singularities or persons. The inconstant constancy, or constant inconstancy, of singularity (or, to introduce another concept we will soon use, *personality*), its metastability and incessant vacillation, cannot be brought to a halt by the political and legal machinery of capture and identity without the exercise and application of incredible degrees of violence. The reality of trans-dividuality does not require a stifling structure of sameness, or the quantification of number, in order to have its *ethos* and perhaps meet the requirements of what even Ricoeur calls 'responsibility' – we will return to this below. Again, to call into the question the concept of the individual does not mean that we have the dividual instead. As Gerald Raunig says, "[i]n the strong substantive sense, 'the dividuum' does not exist" (2016: 121). Discussing the work of Gilbert de la Porrée (ca. 1076–1154), Raunig highlights the concepts of person, individual, and singular. The singular, which "comprises the individual and the person and more" (62) is indeed what we call the trans-dividual. However, it is Gilbert's concept of *dividuum*, "a non-individual singularity" (64), which introduces "a new dimension in which the parts of a non-whole are posited in a non-hierarchical, transversal relation" (65). In this sense, the constant, metastable process tending toward individuation never produces a stable and independent individual – thus, if you will, it ultimately fails in its individuating capacity – and produces instead a singularity as a trans-dividual assemblage.

Ipseity without sameness should not be a problem for the type of thinking we have employed here, which is, as Simondon says, *transductive* thinking. We have already seen this in Chapter Two in particular. For Simondon "the unity of being is a regime of activity that crosses being" throughout, in all its parts (2013: 304). Simondon says, "Being is relation, for the relation is the internal resonance of being in relation to itself" (*ibid.*). With respect to human identity, this relation, this internal resonance, is what can be called *personality*, not in the psychological or moral sense of the stability (or instability) of one's character, but rather in the threshold sense of an aura (in Benjamin's sense) as well as a schematism of the singular and trans-dividual. What is important is the transductive, or threshold-like, character of the relation. Simondon says, "The relation can never be conceived as a relation among preexisting terms, but as a reciprocal regime of exchange of information and causalities within an *individuating* system" (*ibid*; emphasis added). In other words, "the relation expresses the individuation" (*ibid*.). But Simondon also speaks about the subject as he deals with preindividual reality, or the emotions. He says that the emotion does not belong to the individual; rather, it is the exchange, within the subject, between the preindividual potential and the individuated structures (305; I am here paraphrasing Simondon). In this sense, "it prefigures the discovery of the collective" (*ibid*.), and it is thus another way of seeing the relation between the singular and the common. In Chapter Two, we have already noted that for Simondon the singular, "the particular being," is more than the individual (301). What Simondon calls *subject* is the singular, which can be understood as the schematism of personality. In fact, Simondon says that the subject "can be understood as a more or less perfect coherent system of three successive phases of being: preindividual, individuated, and transindividual" (*ibid*.). He very importantly adds, "The subject is not a phase of being opposed to that of the object, but the condensed and systematized unity of the three phases of being" (*ibid*.). As we propose to completely abandon the metaphysics of subjectivity, the language and logic of the subject, we can safely say that Simondon is actually providing us with a description of the singular, under the name of 'subject.' The fact that for Simondon the three phases of being (preindividual, individuated, and transindividual) correspond – not completely, but partially – to what is usually understood as nature, individual, and spirituality, respectively, is still another reason for believing that under the sign of the subject we have something more than the result of either subjection or subjectivation, or both. It is the trans-dividual schematism of singularity that, so to speak, runs through the phases of being and thus produces the unrepeatable and nondenumerable unity of haecceity and personality. In the previous chapter, we saw that Paolo Virno describes Simondon's notion of the subject as "a battlefield" (2004: 78). It is the unresolved tension of trans-dividuality, the constant gathering of forces at the threshold of the common and the singular, their equally constant deterritorialization and dispersal, the never-ending singularization or individuation process, which characterizes the 'battlefield' of the subject – or rather, what no longer is a subject but, precisely, an open singularity.

To go back to Ricoeur, it is his second paradox of identity, the relation between self and other, which may become useful in trying to grasp the reality and meaning of this open singularity. He refers to Leibniz's notion of monadic and, what Ricoeur calls, *"untransferable singularity"* (2016: 247), the notion of an individual substance, as well as the *"multiplicity of perspectives on the world"* (246). This open singularity expresses finitude on the one hand, yet, on the other, it also expresses the universality and infinitude of the common – or rather the 'beyond' and outcast turbulence of the undercommons (Harney and Moten 2013). Just like in Kierkegaard's dialectics of the constantly infinitizing and constantly finitizing movements, we find ourselves beyond the traditional notion of the individual or self. If for Kierkegaard we still have a divided self, the self as a synthesis of two contrary terms, with transductive thinking the deconstruction of the individual or self is even more radical. It is not simply the case that the self is already the other, and the other the self. More importantly, singularity is neither the self nor the other. Singularity is the meaning of the threshold, a 'neither/nor' and, at the same time, a 'both/and.' Essentially, to think singularities against and beyond the politics of number means to think relations without a subject. What we have here is not the Kierkegaardian "singular individual," as Ricoeur says (2016: 247), but rather trans-dividual singularities. Personality, which functions as a sort of schematism within singularity, is not the traditional concept of personality, but a shared (and dockless), collective type of personality; it is singularity's metastable becoming and the translucency of its crossing – the singularity of the imagination, which, as Jason Read says, "is not without relation to the imagination of others" (2016: 252). As Read often notes, this is not a matter of intersubjectivity, but of a network of relations that transcends what appears as a mere group of subjects or individuals. In Read, following Simondon, this is the transindividual dimension; for us, it is the trans-dividual gathering, the open singularization at the threshold of the common. The problem with intersubjectivity, the relationship between self and others, is already clearly explained by Simondon, and we have already seen this in Chapter Two, above. But it is worth repeating it. Simondon says, "The interindividual relation goes from individual to individual; it does not penetrate the individuals; the transindividual action is what makes individuals exist together as elements of a system entailing potentials and metastability, attention and tension" (2013: 294). For him, "individual personalities constitute themselves together through recovery and not through agglomeration" (*ibid.*); namely, through a logic of singularization rather than a reduction to number. Personality "is not based on the amputation of individual differences" (*ibid.*) (that is, trans-dividual features) but on a restructuring of the open, *unresolved*, biological structuring of a living being (295). In this sense, it is the phenomenon of plasticity that, more than any other thing, addresses the paradox of identity, by dissolving it and showing that ipseity (or personality) without sameness is nothing but a description of the threshold trajectory of trans-dividual singularization.

The term 'personality' is used in a very interesting sense for our purpose here by Arnold Gehlen in the final chapter of *Man in the Age of Technology* (1980). Gehlen prepares the ground for his discussion of personality in the previous chapter of his book, on automatisms. I already discussed this in Chapter Three, above, referring to Gehlen's idea of the "immaterial precipitate" of society. Ultimately, Gehlen addresses the question of disindividuation and alienation. It is interesting to note that the German title of his book is *Die Seele im technischen Zeitalter*; thus, the word for 'Man' is 'Soul,' which is also in the title of Franco Berardi's *The Soul at Work* (2009), which, from a different perspective, addresses similar questions and to which I will return shortly. In the chapter on automatisms, Gehlen shows how personality is reduced, through rationalization and bureaucratization (the politics of number), to the figure of the functionary. What is "unwanted," in the domain of specialization, is ultimately singularity. Bureaucratization and machinic assemblage mean *depersonalization* (Gehlen 1980: 152), which is the ethos of the functionary. Gehlen says, "Under such conditions the personality becomes absorbed by the different sets of machinery" (157). He adds that "the specialized functionary, endowed with the specialized training so quickly acquired today, provides no defense against the relapse into barbarism" (158). In his final chapter, he takes issue with the proliferation of subjectivity in modern times and with the "personality-as-subject" becoming "the precipitate" of modern societies (160). But personality is also another word for singularity, which, to be sure, is not used by Gehlen. In fact, for him, personality is "the nonroutine individual, or rather the individual who possesses a larger routine and who is capable of transcending it" (*ibid.*). For Gehlen, this type of individual, which he describes almost as an entrepreneur of the self, becomes "a key figure" (161) in the modern age, thus, we might say, a singularity. Personality names, in fact, "what is qualitatively uncommon" (*ibid.*); namely, what, in our framework, escapes the quantification of number and reaches the threshold of the common, or the undercommons. Thus, Gehlen describes what we mean by singularity using the concept of personality as an immanent schematism: "If we use with emphasis the term 'personality' to denote the ability to produce wondrous effects [which can only happen at the threshold of singularity], then in our own time we should not seek for such effects in the spheres of culture, literature, or the arts, but rather wherever someone seeks to affirm the exacting claims of the spirit within the machinery itself of existence, rather than 'distancing' himself from it" (166; text in brackets added). On the one hand, we have an anticipation of the notion of machinic assemblage in a potentially positive way; on the other, we have the amplification of force, beyond the reductive biopolitics of number, in the domain of the common and everyday life. For Gehlen, this is the making of what we call singularity; he says that "such a person is a personality in this peculiar sense" (*ibid.*). The singular is also what Gehlen calls "most improbable" (*ibid.*). He says, "Today what is most improbable is the capacity of expressing from oneself, in one's activity, more themes, more inspirations than the situation requires, than others expect, than others express" (*ibid.*). Although there is in Gehlen an undue emphasis on individuality and individualism, his concept of personality as a replacement for the sovereign paradigm of modern existence is still fruitful for a thinking that follows the trajectory of the singular and trans-dividual. For Gehlen a personality is "an institution in *one* instance" (*ibid.*; original emphasis). For us, as the schematism of singularity, personality can be the transductive gathering at the threshold of the common, what holds the dividual multitude together, not in a fictional unity, but, to use an expression by Frantz Fanon, in "the ecstasy of dance," in "the dance circle" (2004: 19).

For Franco Berardi, the singularity we are seeking can be seen or founded collectively as "a community no longer dependent on capital" (2009: 44). This is "a human collectivity" that corresponds to, or appears at the threshold of, "the radical inhumanity of the workers' existence" (*ibid.*); thus, it is still a form of disindividuation that yields it, and it is the play between disaffection and care that brings it to the fore. It is a singular humanity (the singular universal, in Sartre's terms), as well as a form of personality (a universal personality) that has nothing to do with individuality or individualism. It is precisely a situation in which *relations without a subject* gather at the threshold of the singular and the common, the trans-dividual amplification of potency. This is what the radical inhumanity of exploitation, alienation, and disaffection can become: a kind of shared or collective personality (which I borrow from the notion of shared mobility in the present economy), capable of founding a singular community, the singularity of the common, by reaching into the undercommons. Berardi says, "It is indeed the estrangement of the workers from their labor, the feeling of alienation and its refusal, that are the bases for a human collectivity autonomous from capital" (44–45). Refusal means active estrangement, namely, the passage from the passivity of alienation to the management of one's power to act. This brings us back to Ricoeur and his third paradox of identity, concerned with responsibility and fragility. He speaks about "the power to act . . . [or] gather one's own life in an intelligible and acceptable narrative" (2016: 250). In this sense, he says that what characterizes human beings is the fact of being "*capable*" (*ibid.*; original emphasis). He sees this capability as expressing various forms of "power-to" (*ibid.*) – and this of course must include, beyond Ricoeur, the collective and shared capacity to transform, or subvert, the community, and build a better society, a better world. Ricoeur himself contrasts all forms of power-to with those "abuses of power exercised as 'power over'" (251). These are forms of sovereign power, sovereign violence, which must be absolutely abolished. But in our view, the abolition of the sovereign and independent individual is an important step in that direction. With that, one also understands the abolition of capitalist relations of production, of whiteness and maleness, of borders, and so on.

Ricoeur speaks of the paradox of human action as one that entails the modalities of both responsibility and fragility. He says, "It is the same person who is responsible and who is fragile" (252). Vico's poetic metaphysics of finitude also emphasizes the importance of human fragility.

Vico calls it "a metaphysics compatible with human frailty" (1988: 109). Although the human being has the capacity to make its own being and the world, this happens in the context of the paradox of freedom/power (responsibility) and fragility – the same fragility of individuation we saw speaking of Stiegler in Chapter Two. Vico says, "Man alone is whatever he chooses to be" (1993: 74). This choice does not happen in a vacuum, and it is not a matter of being absolutely free, which would simply deny the very fact of freedom. As a whole tradition, after Vico, from Marx to Sartre shows, freedom, this complication of the human condition, always happens in a situation. There is no freedom without necessity. Yet, the human life-form (the human being, 'Man,' which must be erased as the absence of an absence, the lack of a lack), is under the compulsion of 'seeing the open,' leaving in despair, with the hope of a return. This is the meaning of choosing and making, the task of becoming, the tension between what one is and can be. The 'whatever' in Vico's "whatever he chooses to be" should be brought back to, and understood in light of, Agamben's analysis we saw in Chapter Four, above, that is, 'whatever' as *the coming being*. Yet, the whatever of freedom is essentially characterized by uncertainty and indeterminacy. What is certain is that for Vico the individuating process is constant and unending, and the individual or self is a made up category. He says, "Nor am I, at the present moment, the same individual I was but a minute ago." And he continues saying that "countless life-instants have already passed by, numberless motions have already taken place, by which I am continuously pushed in the direction of my last day" (1990: 32). Vico is a thinker that could appear as transindividual in his own right in Jason Read's book on transindividuality, alongside Spinoza, Hegel, and Marx, in the sections on transindividual thinkers before Simondon. But for us, he can be better understood as a trans-dividual thinker, a thinker of singularity, as the following quote will show. In *The New Science*, Vico says that "when man understands he extends his mind and takes in the things, but when he does not understand he makes the things out of himself and becomes them by transforming himself into them" (1968: 130). This is indeed a wonderful description of both the notion of machinic assemblage and that of amplification of force, or potency. It is also an ante-litteram insight into the truth of philosophical anthropology we have seen with Gehlen, namely, that the human life-form is characterized by an essential lack, or deficiency. In Vico's poetic and corporeal metaphysics, in his ontology of the convergence of the true and the made, the transformation of the human life-form into the tools and instruments that are made, the extension of the human body to the machinic assemblage is a perfect rendering of the idea of existence as relations without a subject and as trans-dividual gatherings. It is, Vico says, an "imaginative metaphysics," which he opposes to the "rational metaphysics" of the Cartesian tradition. He says that "as rational metaphysics teaches that man becomes all things by understanding them (*homo intelligendo fit omnia*), this imaginative metaphysics shows that man becomes all things by *not* understanding them (*homo non intelligendo fit omnia*)" (*ibid.*). Yet, within this metaphysics of finitude, a metaphysics of bodies, the threshold, the passage to the open remains, for, as Vico says, "what one [can] think is formless and has no limits" (1988: 77; brackets in the original). The human mind "is finite and has a [definite] form" (*ibid.*; brackets in the original). He continues with a prefiguration of Kant's critical philosophy by saying, "Hence, we cannot understand the limitless and formless, though we can think about them" (*ibid.*). The threshold to the open remains because, Vico adds, "As we say in Italian, 'Può andarle raccogliendo, ma non già raccoglierle tutte' (One can keep on picking things up, but never get them all together)" (*ibid.*). 'Picking up,' or 'gathering': the gathering at the threshold thus remains open, and that is, the dialectic between the open and the closed, the infinite and the finite, and so on. In fact, this is the way in which the schematism of personality, the aura of singularity, which is similar to Simondon's notion of internal resonance, is conceived by Kierkegaard as well. Kierkegaard says, "Personhood [or personality] is a synthesis of possibility [or freedom] and necessity" (1980: 40; brackets added). It is equally a synthesis, or a trans-dividual relation, of finitude and infinitude, mystery and manifestation, memory and expectation. Thus it is that the *universalism of difference* we saw in Chapter One, above, becomes meaningful, as the form or figure of *relations without a subject*, the exit from the logic of identity and the metaphysics of subjectivity, the death of the individual and the transposition of the real, the translucency of the singular.

We already noted the formation of heterotopic thresholds speaking about the mirror and the glass in Chapter Six, above. The translucency of the singular is the indeterminacy of the threshold where realization takes place. Alfred North Whitehead speaks of the *translucency of realization* as the metaphysical principle whereby "any eternal object" – which we may here understand as any potentiality – enters an "actual occasion" (1967: 171). This happens because of the force of singularity, or what Nishida Kitarō calls "a single force" (2012: 36) or "an unchanging force that is continually acting" (37). Nishida says this in an essay called "Expressive Activity," where what we here name the threshold of trans-dividuality is understood as the mutual interaction between things that thus "lose their independence" (36). Force itself, or potency, is pre-individual reality as well as the constancy of the individuating process. The occurrence of a single incident, Nishida says, "stands in relation to the entire world" (46), and it is thus a singularity in the sense we have been describing. For Nishida, singularity is "being-at-a-place" (57). This concept has not only a spatial but also a temporal dimension; or rather is it "temporospatial" and "spatiotemporal," as Nishida says in another essay, "The Standpoint of Active Intuition" (84). Indeed, being-at-a-place, in a phenomenological sense, is the situation and instant of expression, the unity of being there and not being there, of capture and exit, of the closed and not closed, in a word, it is a threshold. Even in relation to the self, there is a hiatus of this kind, a 'with,' and a between. As Nishida beautifully says, "there must be a whispering between my mind and my mind" (53). Similarly, we can say, there must be a gathering and a becoming-other, a difference of space and time, an ontological difference, a rupture and a project.

Perhaps the most important concept for us in Nishida's essays is that of the continuity of discontinuity. It is here that the dialectic of time and space, force and time, act and expression, becomes relevant. This is also the dialectic of the situation, being-at-a-place, and the instant, where force, which is the transcendence of time, or "time that possess positive content" (39), shows its immanent and dynamic potency. There is here a convergence of necessity and contingency, of potentiality and actuality, and thus it is not a process that remains within the traditional framework of metaphysics. Indeed, as Nishida says, "the actually existing present determines itself" (64), or "the instant determines the instant itself" (65). This determination, or "self-determination," is "the mediation of the continuity of discontinuity" (67). Nishida says, "Time must therefore be thought as the continuity of discontinuity" (65). The singularity we have been describing in this book, a singularity of the threshold expressing the ontology of unrest, is what Nishida calls "internal unity," similar to the unfolding of the Dao, which we saw in Chapter One, and to Simondon's *internal resonance*. For Nishida, this internal unity means that "a singularity becomes the mediation of singularity itself," or "the singularity mediates the singularity itself" (66). William Haver, the editor and translator of Nishida's book, explains in the glossary that "singularity is 'absolute contradictory self-identity'" (197). Singularity is self-determination, but it is also "that which is determined in relation to that which is not" (*ibid.*); in other words, identity and difference, or, in Hegel's terms, the identity of identity and non-identity. Haver also stresses that for Nishida singularities "are precisely concepts of a threshold" (*ibid.*). But the question of self-determination also touches on the problem around motion, even in the sense of explaining this concept in the context of the theory of the Atomists, Leucippus and Democritus. Is it necessary to explain the source of motion, as Aristotle among others maintains,[1] or can motion be the very expression of the ontology of agitation and unrest, brought about by its own power of mediation, the mediation of the continuity of discontinuity? In the latter sense, motion would be the same as the constant process of individuation that, as we know since Simondon, has no need for a principle external to itself. It is this *internal unity* (Nishida) or *internal resonance* (Simondon) that provides the space/time of the threshold. To be sure, Nishida distinguishes between the mediation of continuity (the threshold of self-awareness) and the mediation of the continuity of discontinuity, that is, a dialectical universal and the threshold of self-activity (86–87). It is this latter form that more closely resembles the idea of the trans-dividual assemblage. It is the self-determination of "the world of historical actuality that . . . expressively determines itself" (95). Nishida speaks of "continuity-qua-discontinuity, discontinuity-qua-continuity" (99). William Haver, in the Glossary to Nishida's volume, says that the word 'qua' translates the Japanese *souk*, common in Chinese and Japanese Buddhist thought, but also bearing "an essential relation to Spinoza's use of *sive* in '*Deus sive Natura*,' variously translated as 'God as Nature' or 'God, or Nature'" (197). Perhaps more importantly for us here, he says that *souk* refers to the coimmanence of two terms, that is, to the fact of relation as transduction" (*ibid.*). Transduction itself is the constant individuating process we have been trying to describe in this book. It is also the meaning of the concept and reality of the threshold. Just like Simondon's concept of transduction, what Stavrides calls "the dynamics of temporal and spatial discontinuity" (2019: 88), as we have seen in Chapter Six, above, which accounts for the ontology of unrest, the ontology of the threshold, is close to Nishida's idea of the historical world as constantly "forming itself," constantly unfolding and "seeing itself" (2012: 136). The historical world itself, as "the self-determination of the eternal now" (*ibid.*) is a threshold, and thus potentially, if we are able to exit its current dystopic state, a heterotopia.

As we move toward the end of this book, we might once again stress the importance of the critique of the concepts of the subject and the independent and sovereign individual. The metaphysics of subjectivity and the construction of the fictional self, a supposedly simple and unified entity, have possibly done a lot of damage not only in the history of philosophy, but in the unfolding of the human adventure. We are at a point in world history where we face genocidal and ecocidal catastrophes of unprecedented proportions. The sovereign individual, master of a free will (as Nietzsche says), is only an impediment to the perhaps not yet lost possibility to turn "away from the abyss," to use Heidegger's language (1971: 92), and set the world on a new course, if that is still possible at all. In addition to the philosophers and philosophical traditions we have reviewed in this book, there are other important experiences and struggles, other thinkers, movements of thought and traditions, which we have not had the chance to consider, but which offer important material and insights for the problems and themes we have considered here: the critique of the individual and the new emphasis on the threshold and trans-dividual reality. One of these is what Cedric Robinson calls the Black radical tradition (Robinson 1983; 2019), which, as my anonymous reviewer points out, has made a four-hundred-year old critique of the individual and subject (p.c.). In Chapter Five, above, we have seen Frantz Fanon's call for the construction of a new humanity as a result of decolonization (2004: 35). This new humanity, the end of oppression, implies the end of subjection and subjectivation, namely, the end of the metaphysics of subjectivity. Indeed, it announces the coming of what is not an entitled subject or sovereign individual. Sadly, we do not have the space to engage with the Black radical tradition, and other 'marginal' (marginalized) traditions, here. We will do so in future work.

NOTE

1. In his *Metaphysics*, speaking of the Atomists, Aristotle says, "For they say that there is always motion. But why it is and what motion it is, they do not state, nor do they give the cause of its being of one sort rather than another" (See Curd 2011: 117). He also says, "Concerning the origin and manner of motion in existing things, these men too, like the rest, lazily neglected to give an account" (111).

Bibliography

Adorno, Theodor W. 1997. *Aesthetic Theory*, trans. Robert Hullot-Kentor. Minneapolis: University of Minnesota Press.
Agamben, Giorgio. 1993. *The Coming Community*, trans. Michael Hardt. Minneapolis: University of Minnesota Press.
———. 1998. *Homo Sacer: Sovereign Power and Bare Life*, trans. Daniel Heller-Roazen. Stanford, CA: Stanford University Press.
———. 2004. *The Open: Man and Animal*, trans. Kevin Attell. Stanford, CA: Stanford University Press.
Alexander, Michelle. 2012 [2010]. *The New Jim Crow: Mass Incarceration in the Age of Colorblindness*, Revised edition. New York: The New Press.
Althusser, Louis, and Étienne Balibar. 1997. *Reading Capital*, trans. Ben Brewster. London: Verso.
Anderson, Bridget. 2000. *Doing the Dirty Work? The Global Politics of Domestic Labour*. New York: Zed Books.
Appiah, Kwame Anthony. 2006. *Cosmopolitanism: Ethics in a World of Strangers*. New York: W. W. Norton & Company.
Aristotle. 1999. *Nicomachean Ethics*, trans. Terence Irwin. Indianapolis, IN: Hackett.
Bachelard, Gaston. 1964. *The Poetics of Space*, trans. Maria Jolas. Boston: Beacon Press.
———. 1971. *The Poetics of Reverie: Childhood, Language, and the Cosmos*, trans. Daniel Russell. Boston: Beacon Press.
Balibar, Étienne. 2002. *Politics and the Other Scene*, trans. Christine Jones, James Swenson, and Chris Turner. London: Verso.
———. 2014. *Equaliberty: Political Essays*, trans. James Ingram. Durham, NC: Duke University Press.
———. 2015. *Violence and Civility: On the Limits of Political Philosophy*, trans. G. M. Goshgarian. New York: Columbia University Press.
Benjamin, Walter. 1968. "Theses on the Philosophy of History." In *Illuminations*, trans. Harry Zohn. New York: Shocken Books.
———. 1968a. "On Some Motifs in Baudelaire." In *Illuminations*, trans. Harry Zohn. New York: Shocken Books.
———. 1978. "Critique of Violence." In *Reflections*, trans. Edmund Jephcott. New York: Shocken Books.
———. 1999. *The Arcades Project*, trans. Howard Eiland and Kevin McLaughlin. Cambridge, MA: Harvard University Press.
Berardi, Franco. 2009. *The Soul at Work: From Alienation to Autonomy*, trans. Francesca Cadel and Giuseppina Mecchia. 2009. Los Angeles: Semiotext(e).
Blake, Nancy. 1985. "The Word as Truth or Delirium: Faulkner's *As I Lay Dying*." *Revue Belge de Philologie e d'Histoire*, tome 63, fasc. 3, 554–563.
Bobbio, Norberto. 1987. *Which Socialism?*, trans. Roger Griffin. Minneapolis: University of Minnesota Press.
Boltanski, Luc, and Ève Chiapello. 2018. *The New Spirit of Capitalism*, trans. Gregory Elliott. London: Verso.
Bubeck, Diemut Elizabeth. 1995. *Care, Gender, and Justice*. Oxford: Clarendon Press.
Cadava, Eduardo, Peter Connor, and Jean-Luc Nancy (eds.). 1991. *Who Comes after the Subject?* New York: Routledge.
Carré, Louis. 2013. "Bertrand Ogilvie, 2012, *L'Homme jetable. Essai sur l'exterminisme et la violence extrême*, Paris, Éditions Amsterdam, 137 p. & Bertrand Ogilvie, 2012, *La*

Seconde Nature du politique. Essai d'anthropologie négative, Paris, L'Harmattan, 'La Philosophie en commune', 174 p.," *Revue européenne des sciences sociales* [En ligne], 51-1.
Chuang Tzu. 2006. *The Book of Chuang Tzu,* trans. Martin Palmer with Elizabeth Breuilly, Chang Wai Ming, and Jay Ramsay. London: Penguin Books.
Confucius. 2000. *The Analects,* trans. Raymond Dawson. Oxford: Oxford University Press.
Curcio, Renato. 2018. *L'algoritmo sovrano: metamorfosi identitarie e rischi totalitari nella società artificiale.* Rome: Sensibili alle foglie.
Curd, Patricia. 2011. *A Presocratics Reader: Selected Fragments and Testimonia,* trans. Richard D. McKirahan and Patricia Curd. Indianapolis, IN: Hackett.
Dalla Costa, Mariarosa, and Selma James. 1972. *The Power of Women and the Subversion of the Community.* Bristol, UK: Falling Wall Press.
Davis, Angela. 2003. *Are Prisons Obsolete?* New York: Seven Stories Press.
Debord, Guy. 1995. *The Society of the Spectacle,* trans. Donald Nicholson-Smith. New York: Zone Books.
Deleuze, Gilles. 1995. *Negotiations: 1972–1990,* trans. Martin Joughin. New York: Columbia University Press.
Deleuze, Gilles, and Félix Guattari. 1987. *A Thousand Plateaus: Capitalism and Schizophrenia,* trans. Brian Massumi. Minneapolis: University of Minnesota Press.
Derrida, Jacques. 1988. *Limited Inc,* trans. Jeffrey Mehlman and Samuel Weber. Evanston, IL: Northwestern University Press.
Descartes, René. 1993. *Meditations on First Philosophy,* 3rd edition, trans. Donald A. Cress. Indianapolis, IN: Hackett.
Duns Scotus, John. 1987. *Philosophical Writings,* trans. Allan Wolter. Indianapolis, IN: Hackett.
Evans, Brad, and Henry A. Giroux. 2015. *Disposable Futures: The Seduction of Violence in the Age of Spectacle.* Open Media Series. San Francisco: City Lights Books.
Fanon, Frantz. 2004. *The Wretched of the Earth,* trans. Richard Philcox, with a foreword by Homi K. Bhabha and a preface by Jean-Paul Sartre. New York: Grove Press.
Faulkner, William. 1987 (1930). *As I Lay Dying.* New York: Vintage Books.
Federici, Silvia. 2012. *Revolution at Point Zero: Housework, Reproduction, and Feminist Struggle.* Oakland, CA: PM Press.
Florida, Richard. 2003. *The Rise of the Creative Class.* New York: Basic Books.
Foucault, Michel. 1977. *Discipline and Punish: The Birth of the Prison,* trans. Alan Sheridan. New York: Vintage.
———. 1988. *The Care of the Self.* Volume 3 of *The History of Sexuality,* trans. Robert Hurley. New York: Vintage Books.
———. 1997. *"Society Must Be Defended." Lectures at the Collège de France, 1975–1976,* trans. David Macey. New York: Picador.
———. 1998. "Different Spaces." In *Essential Works of Foucault, 1954–1984.* Volume 2: *Aesthetics, Method, and Epistemology.* Edited by James D. Faubion; translated by Robert Hurley and others. New York: The New Press.
———. 2010. *The Government of Self and Others. Lectures at the Collège de France, 1982–1983,* trans. Graham Burchell. New York: Picador.
Gehlen, Arnold. 1980. *Man in the Age of Technology,* trans. Patricia Lipscomb. New York: Columbia University Press.
———. 1988. *Man: His Nature and Place in the World,* trans. Clare McMillan and Karl Pillemer. New York: Columbia University Press.
Gilman-Opalsky, Richard. 2014. *Precarious Communism: Manifest Mutations, Manifesto Detourned.* New York: Minor Compositions.
Gramsci, Antonio. 1971. *Selections from the Prison Notebooks,* trans. Quintin Hoare and Geoffrey Nowell Smith. New York: International Publishers.
Guattari, Félix. 1985. "Singularité et complexité," Seminar of January 22, 1985, at https://www.revue-chimeres.fr/IMG/pdf/1._22-01-85_felix_guattari_singularite_et_complexite.pdf (accessed on 9/30/2019).

———. 2016. *Lines of Flight: For Another World of Possibilities*, trans. Andrew Goffey. London: Bloomsbury Academic.
Gullì, Bruno. 2005. *Labor of Fire: The Ontology of Labor between Economy and Culture*. Philadelphia: Temple University Press.
———. 2005a. "The Folly of Utopia: A Contribution to the Critique of Cultural Disorder," in *Situations: Project of the Radical Imagination*. Vol. 1, No. 1 (April 2005): 161–191.
———. 2010. *Earthly Plenitudes: A Study on Sovereignty and Labor*. Philadelphia: Temple University Press.
———. 2014. *Humanity and the Enemy: How Ethics Can Rid Politics of Violence*. New York: Palgrave Macmillan.
Haesler, Aldo J. 1995. *Sociologie de l'argent et postmodernité: Recherche sur le conséquences sociales et culturelles de l'électronisation des flux monétaires*. Geneva: Librairie Droz.
Han, Byung-Chul. 2018. *The Expulsion of the Other: Society, Perception and Communication Today*, trans. Wieland Hoban. Cambridge, UK: Polity Press.
Hardt, Michael, and Antonio Negri. 2017. *Assembly*. Oxford: Oxford University Press.
Harney, Stefano, and Fred Moten. 2013. *The Undercommons: Fugitive Planning and Black Studies*. New York: Autonomedia.
Harvey, David. 2003. *The New Imperialism*. Oxford: Oxford University Press.
Hegel, Georg Wilhelm Friedrich. 1995. *Lectures on the History of Philosophy: Greek Philosophy to Plato*, Volume I, trans. E. S. Haldane. Lincoln: University of Nebraska Press.
Heidegger, Martin. 1971. *Poetry, Language, Thought*, trans. Albert Hofstadter. New York: Harper and Row.
———. 1975. *Early Greek Thinking*, trans. David Farrell Krell and Frank A. Capuzzi. San Francisco: Harper & Row.
———. 1977. *The Question Concerning Technology and Other Essays*, trans. William Lovitt. New York: Harper & Row.
———. 1977a. "Letter on Humanism," in *Basic Writings*, ed. D. F. Krell. New York: Harper and Row.
———. 1996a. *Hölderlin's Hymn "The Ister,"* trans. William McNeill and Julia Davis. Bloomington: Indiana University Press.
———. 1996b. *Being and Time*, trans. Joan Stambaugh. New York: State University of New York Press.
Hobbes, Thomas. 1994. *Leviathan*, ed. Edwin Curley. Indianapolis, IN: Hackett Publishing Company.
Jaspers, Karl. 2010. *The Origin and Goal of History*. New York: Routledge.
Kierkegaard, Søren. 1980. *The Sickness unto Death*, trans. Howard V. Hong and Edna H. Hong. Princeton, NJ: Princeton University Press.
———. 1985. *Fear and Trembling*, trans. Alastair Hannay. New York: Penguin Books.
Kittay, Eva Feder. 1999. *Love's Labor: Essays on Women, Equality, and Dependency*. New York: Routledge.
Laozi. 1954. *Tao Te Ching: The Book of the Way and Its Virtue*, trans. Julius Lodewijk Duyvendak. London: John Murray.
———. 2002. *The Daodejing of Laozi*, trans. Philip J. Ivanhoe. Indianapolis, IN: Hackett.
Lazzarato, Maurizio. 2012. *The Making of the Indebted Man: An Essay on the Neoliberal Condition*, trans. Joshua David Jordan. Los Angeles: Semiotext(e).
———. 2014. *Signs and Machines: Capitalism and the Production of Subjectivity*, trans. Joshua David Jordan. Los Angeles: Semiotext(e).
Leibniz, G. W. 1972. *Political Writings*, ed. Patrick Riley. Cambridge: Cambridge University Press.
———. 1989. "Discourse on Metaphysics." In *Philosophical Essays*, trans. Roger Aries and Daniel Garber. Indianapolis, IN: Hackett.
Lordon, Frédéric. 2014. *Willing Slaves of Capital: Spinoza and Marx on Desire*, trans. Gabriel Ash. London: Verso.
Lucretius. 2001. *On the Nature of Things*, trans. Martin Ferguson Smith. Indianapolis, IN: Hackett.

Machiavelli, Niccolò. 1950. *The Prince and the Discourses*. New York: Random House.
Malabou, Catherine. 2012. *Ontology of the Accident: An Essay on Destructive Plasticity*, trans. Carolyn Shread. Cambridge, UK: Polity Press.
Marramao, Giacomo. 2012. *The Passage West: Philosophy after the Age of the Nation State*, trans. Matteo Mandarini. London: Verso.
Marx, Karl. 1973. *Grundrisse: Foundations of the Critique of Political Economy*, trans. Martin Nicolaus. New York: Vintage Books.
———. 1975. "Economic and Philosophical Manuscripts," in *Early Writings*, trans. Rodney Livingston and Gregor Brenton. New York: Vintage Books.
———. 1975a. "Concerning Feuerbach," in *Early Writings*, trans. Rodney Livingston and Gregor Brenton. New York: Vintage Books.
———. 1977. *Capital, Vol. I*, trans. Ben Fowkes. New York: Vintage.
Mezzadra, Sandro, and Brett Neilson. 2013. *Border as Method, or, the Multiplication of Labor*. Durham, NC: Duke University Press.
———. 2019. *The Politics of Operations: Excavating Contemporary Capitalism*. Durham, NC: Duke University Press.
Miquel, Paul-Antoine. 2019. *Vénus et Prométhée: Essai sur la relation entre l'humain et la biosphère*. Paris: Éditons Kimé.
Morgan, George, and Pariece Nelligan. 2018. *The Creativity Hoax: Precarious Work and the Gig Economy*. London: Anthem Press.
Morini, Cristina. 2010. *Per amore o per forza: Femminilizzazione del lavoro e biopolitiche del corpo*. Verona: Ombre corte.
Mouffe, Chantal. 2005. *The Return of the Political*. London: Verso.
Mumford, Lewis. 2000. (1952). *Art and Technics*. New York: Columbia University Press.
Nancy, Jean-Luc. 1993. *The Experience of Freedom*, trans. Bridget McDonald. Stanford, CA: Stanford University Press.
———. 2000. *Being Singular Plural*, trans. Robert D. Richardson and Anne E. O'Byrne. Stanford, CA: Stanford University Press.
Nietzsche, Friedrich. 1967. *On the Genealogy of Morals* and *Ecce Homo*, trans. Walter Kaufmann. New York: Random House.
———. 1968. *The Will to Power*, trans. Walter Kaufmann. New York: Random House.
———. 1978. *Thus Spoke Zarathustra: A Book for All and None*, trans. Walter Kaufmann. New York: Penguin Books.
———. 1990. *The Twilight of the Idols / The Anti-Christ*, trans. R. J. Hollingdale. New York: Penguin Books.
Nishida, Kitarō. 2012. *Ontology of Production. 3 Essays*. Translated and with an Introduction by William Haver. Durham, NC: Duke University Press.
Nussbaum, Martha C. 2006. *Frontiers of Justice: Disability, Nationality, Species Membership*. Cambridge, MA: Harvard University Press.
Ogilvie, Bertrand. 2012. *L'Homme jetable. Essai sur l'exterminisme et la violence extreme*. Paris: Éditions Amsterdam.
Pasqualotto, Giangiorgio. 1988. "Azione senza forzature: 'Wu-wei' di Gramsci," in *Belfagor*, 4 (1988), 452–456.
Pasquinelli, Matteo. 2014. "Capitalismo macchinico e plusvalore di rete. Note sull'economia politica della macchina di Turing." In Matteo Pasquinelli, ed., *Gli algoritmi del capitale. Accelerazionismo, macchine della conoscenza e autonomia del comune*. Verona: Ombre Corte.
Pellerin, Ananda. 2019. "Baloji's Incredible New Film Confronts Zombie Culture and Shared Isolation," in *Dazed*. March 14.
Pradeu, Thomas. 2012. *The Limits of the Self: Immunology and Biological Identity*, trans. Elizabeth Vitanza. New York: Oxford University Press.
Rancière, Jacques. 1999. *Dis-Agreement: Politics and Philosophy*, trans. J. Rose. Minneapolis: University of Minnesota Press.
Raunig, Gerald. 2010. *A Thousand Machines: A Concise Philosophy of the Machine as Social Movement*, trans. Aileen Derieg. Los Angeles: Semiotext(e).

———. 2016. *Dividuum: Machinic Capitalism and Molecular Revolution*, trans. Aileen Derieg. Los Angeles: Semiotext(e).
Read, Jason. 2016. *The Politics of Transindividuality*. Leiden: Brill.
Ricoeur, Paul. 2016. *Philosophical Anthropology*, trans. David Pellauer. Cambridge, UK: Polity Press.
Rimbaud, Arthur. 2008. *Complete Works*, trans. Paul Schmidt. New York: HarperCollins Publishers.
Robinson, Cedric J. 1983. *Black Marxism: The Making of the Black Radical Tradition*. Chapel Hill: The University of North Carolina Press.
———. 2019. *On Racial Capitalism, Black Internationalism, and Cultures of Resistance*. London: Pluto Press.
Saro-Wiwa, Ken. 1994. *Sozaboy: A Novel in Rotten English*. New York: Longman African Writers.
Sartre, Jean-Paul. "Existentialism," in *Existentialism and Human Emotions*, trans. Bernard Frechtman. New York: Kensington Publishing Corp.
Sholette, Gregory. 2010. *Dark Matter: Art and Politics in the Age of Enterprise Culture*. London: Pluto Press.
Shukaitis, Stevphen. 2016. *The Composition of Movements to Come*. London: Rowman & Littlefield.
Sibertin-Blanc, Guillaume. 2016. *State and Politics: Deleuze and Guattari on Marx*, trans. Ames Hodges. South Pasadena, CA: Semiotext(e).
Simondon, Gilbert. 2011. *Two Lessons on Animal and Man*, trans. Drew S. Burk. Minneapolis: Univocal Publishing.
———. 2013 [1re édition 2005]. *L'individuation à la lumière des notions de forme e d'information*. Grenoble: Éditions Jérôme Millon.
Spinoza, Baruch. 1992. *Ethics*, trans. Samuel Shirley. Indianapolis, IN: Hackett Publishing Company.
———. 2000. *Political Treatise*, trans. Samuel Shirley. Indianapolis, IN: Hackett Publishing Company.
Srniceck, Nick. 2017. *Platform Capitalism*. Cambridge, UK: Polity Press.
Stavrides, Stavros. 2007. "Heterotopias and the Experience of Porous Urban Space." In *Loose Space: Possibility and Diversity in Urban Life*, edited by Karen Franck and Quentin Stevens. London: Routledge.
———. 2019. *Towards the City of Thresholds*. Brooklyn, NY: Common Notions.
Stiegler, Bernard. 2009. "The Theater of Individuation: Phase-Shift and Resolution in Simondon and Heidegger," trans. Kristina Lebedeva. *Parrhesia*, Number 7, 46–57.
———. 2010. *For a New Critique of Political Economy*, trans. Daniel Ross. Cambridge, UK: Polity Press.
———. 2013. *Uncontrollable Societies of Disaffected Individuals*, trans. Daniel Ross. Cambridge, UK: Polity Press.
Vico, Giambattista. 1968. *The New Science*, trans. Thomas Goddard Bergin and Max Harold Fisch. Ithaca, NY: Cornell University Press.
———. 1988. *On the Most Ancient Wisdom of the Italians Unearthed from the Origins of the Latin Language. Book One: Metaphysics*, trans. L. M. Palmer. Ithaca, NY: Cornell University Press.
———. 1990. *On the Study Methods of Our Time*, trans. Elio Gianturco. Ithaca, NY: Cornell University Press.
———. 1993. *On Humanistic Education (Six Inaugural Orations, 1699–1707)*, trans. Giorgio A. Pinton and Arthur W. Shippee. Ithaca, NY: Cornell University Press.
Virno. Paolo. 2004. *A Grammar of the Multitude: For an Analysis of Contemporary Forms of Life*, trans. Isabella Bertoletti, James Cascaito, and Andrea Casson. Los Angeles: Semiotext(e).
———. 2009. "Angels and the General Intellect: Individuation in Duns Scotus and Gilbert Simondon," trans. Nick Heron. *Parrhesia*, Number 7, 58–67.
Vitale, Alex S. 2017. *The End of Policing*. London: Verso.

Whitehead, Alfred North. 1967. *Science and the Modern World*. New York: The Free Press.
Willis, Paul. 1977. *Learning to Labor: How Working Class Kids Get Working Class Jobs*. New York: Columbia University Press.
Žukauskaitė, Audronė. 2011. "Ethics between Particularity and Universality," in *Deleuze and Ethics*, ed. Nathan Jun and Daniel W. Smith. Edinburgh: Edinburgh University Press.

Index

accident: ontology of the, 5, 61–64, 91, 92, 92–94
Adorno, Theodor W., 115
Agamben, Giorgio, 20–21, 55, 61–64, 70, 71, 88–89, 138–140
Alexander, Michelle, 75
algorithm, 37–38, 55–57, 61–64, 115–117, 123–124
alienation, 1, 4, 39–40, 43, 55, 58–60, 61–64, 70–71, 89–90, 111, 115–117
Althusser, Louis, 21–22, 43
anarchism, 127–128
anarchy: philosophy of, 14–16
Anaxagoras, 93
Anaximander, 18–20, 45, 84, 127, 128
Anaximenes, 45, 77–78
antiviolence, 68–70, 72–75, 79–81, 88, 96. *See also* civility
Appiah, Kwame Anthony, 11–12
Aristotle, 21–22, 143n1
art, 3–4, 18–20, 21, 55, 79, 89–90, 101, 103–104, 104–105, 105–106, 110, 113–115; and labor, 5, 101, 103, 105–117
assemblage. *See* trans-dividual assemblage; machinic assemblage
aura, 1–2, 25–27, 89–90, 134, 138–140. *See also* personality; schematism

Bachelard, Gaston, 4, 14–21
Balibar, Étienne, 11, 16, 21–22, 64, 71–77, 79, 85, 86, 112
Baloji, 55–57
Bartolini, Luigi, 124–125
Bauman, Zygmunt, 70
becoming, 1, 14, 24, 25–27, 29, 30, 39, 43–44, 45, 46, 55–57, 58–60, 61–64, 72–75, 83, 84, 87–88, 92, 93, 119, 135–136, 138–140

Benjamin, Walter, 21, 67–75, 79–81, 88–89, 89–90, 96, 134
Bentham, Jeremy, 34–35
Berardi, Franco, 136–138
biopolitics, 5, 40–41, 48, 70, 75–78, 136–138. *See also* control society; politics of number
Black Lives Matter, 61–64
Blake, Nancy, 33
Bobbio, Norberto, 32
Boltanski, Luc, 115
border, 5, 16–18, 53, 55–57, 58–60, 61–64, 70, 75, 85, 93–94, 110–113, 115–117
Bratsis, Peter, 123–124
Bubeck, Elizabeth Diemut, 127–128
Buddhism, 12–13, 127–128
Burnet, Macfarlane, 48

capitalism, 55, 57–58, 67, 86, 87–88, 96, 103, 106–107, 121–122
capture, 1, 5, 12–13, 14, 16, 18–21, 37–38, 41, 43, 48, 53–55, 57–64, 68–70, 72–75, 85, 86–89, 91–92, 92, 93–94, 95, 96, 103, 111, 133, 140–141; exit from, 5, 41, 60–61, 72–75, 124–125
care, 3–4, 5, 14–16, 42–43, 68–70, 75–77, 79–81, 101, 104, 108, 111, 113–115, 122–131; of the self, 14–16, 79; workers, 111–112
Carré, Louis, 77–78
Chiapello, Ève, 115
Christianity, 127–128
Chuang Tzu. *See* Zhuangzi
civility, 68–70, 71–77, 79–81, 88, 96
Cohen, Leonard, 21–22
the common, 17, 24–29, 31, 38–40, 47, 49–50, 53–55, 57–64, 71–72, 84, 87–88, 93–94, 95, 96, 101, 104, 105,

108–110, 113, 120, 123–131, 134–135, 136–138; threshold of the, 1, 2
communism, 87–88, 127–128
Confucius, 14–16
contingency, 1, 4, 10–11, 13, 14, 21–22, 49–50, 50n2, 58–60, 90–91, 93, 105, 123, 125–127, 141
counterviolence, 96
cruelty. *See* exterminism; violence
Curcio, Renato, 55–57

Dalla Costa, Mariarosa, 117n8
Daoism, 14
Davis, Angela, 75–77
Debord, Guy, 68, 106, 108
de-disindividuation, 55, 55–57, 58–60
Deleuze, Gilles, 16, 37, 37–38, 47, 58, 79, 83, 84–89, 92, 124–125, 133
Democritus, 141
dependency, 2, 3, 128–131
Derrida, Jacques, 11–12, 72–75
Descartes, René, 43–46, 49, 55–57
dialectic, 4, 13–14, 33, 49–50, 68–70, 72–75, 89, 140, 141
disaffection, 1, 3–4, 5, 43, 55, 58–61, 121–123, 125–127, 129–131, 138
disindividuation, 1, 3–4, 32, 33, 34–35, 39–40, 42, 43, 53, 55, 58–60, 72–77, 79, 120–121, 123, 125, 136, 138
disposability, 5, 70–71, 75–77, 79–81, 103
dividuality, 3, 44–45, 58–60, 123, 133
Duns Scotus, John, 10–11, 27, 47, 84
Duyvendak, Lodevijk, 10–11

Empedocles, 77–78
Evans, Brad, 67–75
exterminism, 5, 77, 78–79

Fanon, Frantz, 67–70, 72–75, 79, 142
Faulkner, William, 33
Federici, Silvia, 117n8
Fenner, Frank, 48
Fenves, Peter, 115
Fichte, Johann Gottlieb, 64
Finer, Herman, 39
Florida, Richard, 106
Foucault, Michel, 14–16, 34–35, 40–41, 53, 60, 70–71, 72, 75, 77–78, 79, 90–91, 96, 106–107, 121–122, 124–125
Freire, Paulo, 67

Garner, Eric, 68
gathering threshold, 3–4, 53, 64, 71–77, 79, 83, 90–91, 125–127, 129–131
Gehlen, Arnold, 20, 40, 128–129, 136–138, 138–140
Gilets Jaunes, 58, 117n10
Gilets Noirs, 58, 64
Gilman-Opalsky, Richard, 58–61
Giroux, Henry, 67–75
Gramsci, Antonio, 12–13
Green, André, 16
Guattari, Félix, 16, 37, 38, 47, 58, 79, 83, 84–89, 92, 94, 95, 119, 124–125, 133

Haesler, Aldo J., 37–38, 53–55, 55
Han, Byung-Chul, 55, 89
Hardy, Oliver, 33–34
Hardt, Michael, 71–72, 106–110, 112–113, 115
Harney, Stefano, 39–40, 135
Harvey, David, 67–68
Haver, William, 141–142
Hegel, Georg Wilhelm Friedrich, 14, 46, 68–70, 72–75, 78, 125–127, 138–140, 141
Heidegger, Martin, 18–21, 32, 37, 41–44, 49, 84–85, 93, 101, 110, 122, 125–129, 142
Heraclitus, 14, 18–20, 29, 37, 45, 46, 77–78, 92–93, 122
Hobbes, Thomas, 112–113
Hölderlin, Friedrich, 41–42
Husserl, Edmond, 125

individuality, 3, 4, 24–25, 27, 33, 34–35, 47, 48, 53, 55, 68, 72–75, 79–81
individuation, 2, 4, 21–22, 23–33, 37, 38, 43, 46–47, 61–64, 72–75, 79, 84, 92–93, 95, 102–103, 119, 119–123, 125–127, 133–135; dignity of, 61–64, 113–115; fragility of, 32, 138–140; impossible, 11–12, 25–27, 33–34, 84; loss of, 32, 122; process of, 1, 2, 24–25, 27, 29, 31, 38, 77–78, 94, 119, 120, 134–135, 141; transindividual, 39, 48–49

Institute for the Radical Imagination, 123–124
intersubjectivity, 2, 3, 72–75, 94–95, 135–136
Ivanhoe, Philip J., 10–11
Izambard, Georges, 50n1

James, Selma, 117n8
Jaspers, Karl, 10

Kafka, Franz, 92
Kant, Immanuel, 138–140
Kierkegaard, Søren, 37–38, 43–44, 49, 68, 135–136, 138–140
Kittay, Eva Feder, 3, 129

labor: art and, 5, 101, 103, 107–117; living, 110, 112, 113, 115–117
Lacan, Jacques, 33
Laozi, 4, 10, 11, 12–13, 14, 14–16, 17, 84
Latouche, Serge, 22n1
Laurel, Stanley, 33–34
Lazzarato, Maurizio, 37–40, 55, 94, 95, 105–107, 112–113, 115
Leibniz, Gottfried Wilhelm, 2, 10–11, 14, 21–22, 88, 95, 119, 135
Lenin, Vladimir, 72
Leopardi, Giacomo, 21–22
Leucippus, 141
Levi, Primo, 68
Locke, John, 43–44, 49
Lordon, Frédéric, 57, 58, 60–61, 68, 72, 79, 103, 111, 123–124
love, 3–4, 68–70, 88, 123, 124–125
Lucretius, 11–12, 21–22
Luhmann, Niklas, 9
Luxemburg, Rosa, 72

Machiavelli, Niccolò, 60–61, 87–88
machinic assemblage, 30–31, 37–38, 105, 115–117, 124–125, 136–138, 138–140
Malabou, Catherine, 61, 91, 92, 92–94
Marramao, Giacomo, 3–4, 9–10, 17
Marx, Karl, 17, 38, 46, 47–48, 58–60, 67–68, 72, 94–95, 103, 104, 104–105, 105–106, 107–108, 115, 120–121, 124–125, 129, 138–140
Mediterranea - Saving Humans, 64

Melville, Herman, 14–16
metastability, 24–25, 28, 31, 43–44, 133–134, 135–136
Mezzadra, Sandro, 64, 85, 86, 94–95, 96, 111–112, 113
migration, 58–60, 64, 70, 75, 86, 129
Miquel, Paul-Antoine, 11–12, 25–27
Morgan, George, 101, 106–107, 110, 111, 112–115
Morini, Cristina, 113–115
Moten, Fred, 39–40, 135
Mouffe Chantal, 96
Mumford, Lewis, 10

Nancy, Jean-Luc, 33–34, 115
Negri, Antonio, 32, 71–72, 96, 106–110, 112–113, 115, 117n10
Neilson, Brett, 64, 85, 86, 94–95, 96, 111–112, 113
Nelligan, Pariece, 101, 106–107, 110, 111, 112–115
neoliberalism, 25–27, 67, 110
Nietzsche, Friedrich, 23, 38, 39, 40–41, 44–45, 49–50, 55–57, 71, 101, 104, 104–105, 142
Nishida, Kitarō, 11–12, 16–17, 131n1, 140–142
Nussbaum, Martha, 129

Ogilvie, Bertrand, 77–79
Orta, Ramsey, 68

Parmenides, 14, 18–20, 29, 31, 43, 45, 46, 50n2, 119–120
Pasqualotto, Giangiorgio, 12–13
Pasquinelli, Matteo, 124–125
Pelias, Michael, 35n3, 123–124
personality, 1–2, 3, 30–31, 39–40, 133–138. *See also* aura; schematism
plasticity, 3, 25–27, 91, 92, 93–95, 121–122, 135–136
politics of number, 1, 2, 5, 32, 37–38, 48, 58–60, 64, 71–72, 78–79, 83–84, 101, 127, 129–131, 135–138. *See also* biopolitics
Porrée, Gilbert de la, 133–134
Pradeu, Thomas, 46–50
the preindividual, 23, 24–30, 33, 34–35, 40–41, 53, 53–55, 57–60, 103,

125–127, 134–135
Pythagoreans, 125–127

Qin Shi Huangdi, 14–16

Rancière, Jacques, 58, 112
Raunig, Gerald, 37–38, 115–117, 124–125, 133–134
Read, Jason, 3, 27, 72–75, 101, 102, 103, 135–136, 138–140
Ricoeur, Paul, 18, 125, 133–134, 135–136, 138
Rimbaud, Arthur, 43–44, 50n1
Robertson, Roland, 9–10
Robinson, Cedric, 142

Said, Edward, 10
Saro-Wiwa, Ken, 122–123
Sartre, Jean-Paul, 41, 42, 43–44, 138, 138–140
schematism, 1–2, 25–27, 30–31, 134–140. *See also* aura; personality
Sen, Amartya, 129
Shelley, Percy Bysshe, 18
Sholette, Gregory, 107–108
Shukaitis, Stevphen, 103, 107
Sibertin-Blanc, Guillaume, 87
Sica, Vittorio de, 124–125
Silicon Valley, 110
Simondon, Gilbert, 2, 11–12, 21–22, 23–33, 39, 46, 46–47, 48–49, 61, 77–78, 83, 88, 115, 119, 120–122, 133, 134–136, 138–140, 141
Simplicius, 18–20
singularization, 28–29, 37, 38–39, 53–55, 57–58, 61–64, 68–70, 95, 96, 123–125, 129–131, 134–136
Sophocles, 123–124
Spinoza, Baruch, 11, 21–22, 23–24, 46, 49, 53, 61, 77–78, 79, 101, 103, 115, 124–125, 138–140, 141–142
Srnicek, Nick, 55
Stavrides, Stavros, 88–91, 141–142
Stiegler, Bernard, 24–25, 30, 32, 42, 120–125, 128–129, 138–140
Supervielle, Jules, 16, 17–18

Taoism, 127–128. *See also* Daoism
Thales, 45
trans-dividuality, 2, 3, 9, 13–14, 16–17, 27, 33, 47, 58–60, 61–64, 72–75, 83, 89, 89–90, 94, 112–113, 120–121, 124–125, 128–129, 131n1, 133, 134–135, 140. *See also* trans-dividuation
trans-dividuation, 1, 14, 30, 32, 33, 33–34, 101, 102–103, 105, 120–121
transduction, 24–25, 28–29, 31, 32–33, 33–34, 83, 120–121, 141–142
transindividuality, 2, 3, 4, 35n1, 72–75, 84, 89, 102, 103, 120–121, 122–123, 138–140. *See also* transindividuation
transindividuation, 1, 3, 23, 28, 29, 32, 101, 102
Tronti, Mario, 96

ubuntu, 123–124, 129
undercommons, 39–40, 135, 136–138
Uexküll, Jacob von, 20–21

Vico, Giambattista, 3–4, 41–42, 44–45, 55, 58–60, 104, 138–140
violence, 64, 67–68, 71–81, 89, 96, 127–129, 133–134; biopolitical, 70, 75–77; (as capture), 18–20, 48; critique of, 67; extreme, 5, 75, 77, 78–79; institutional, 64, 68–70, 75–77; normalization of, 68–71; police, 48, 75–77; sovereign, 61, 71, 138; State, 85, 86–87; structural, 86
Virno, Paolo, 24–28, 95, 119, 119–122, 131n1, 134–135
Vitale, Alex, 75–77

Whitehead, Alfred North, 140
Willis, Paul, 103

Zapatistas, 18
Zeno, 34–35
Zhuangzi, 4, 12–13, 16, 55–57
Žukauskaitė, Audronė, 87–88

About the Author

Bruno Gullì is the author of various articles and three books, including *Labor of Fire: The Ontology of Labor between Economy and Culture* (2005). He teaches philosophy at CUNY-Kingsborough in Brooklyn, NY.